THE NEW AMERICAN WAR FILM

THE NEW AMERICAN WAR FILM

ROBERT BURGOYNE

University of Minnesota Press
Minneapolis
London

A portion of chapter 1 was previously published in a different form in "Embodiment in the War Film: *Paradise Now* and *The Hurt Locker*," in "War and the Body," ed. Kevin McSorley and Sarah Maltby, special issue, *War and Culture Studies* 5, no. 1 (July 2012): 7–19. A portion of chapter 2 was published in a different form in "The Violated Body: Affect and Somatic Intensity in *Zero Dark Thirty*," in *The Philosophy of War Films*, ed. David LaRocca (Lexington: University Press of Kentucky, 2015), 247–60; copyright 2014 by the University Press of Kentucky; the piece is adapted here with permission. A portion of chapter 5 was previously published in a different form in "Postheroic War / The Body at Risk," in *Disappearing War: Interdisciplinary Perspectives on Cinema and Erasure in the Post 9/11 World*, ed. Christina Hellmich and Lisa Purse (Edinburgh: Edinburgh University Press, 2017), 56–72.

Published by the University of Minnesota Press
111 Third Avenue South, Suite 290
Minneapolis, MN 55401–2520
http://www.upress.umn.edu

ISBN 978-1-5179-1543-8 (hc)
ISBN 978-1-5179-1544-5 (pb)

LC record available at https://lccn.loc.gov/2023012248

Printed on acid-free paper

UMP KEP

To the memory of my father-in-law, Eli Shaban, an organic intellectual who never lost his curiosity and his interest in the larger world

CONTENTS

INTRODUCTION

THE GREAT SCHOLAR OF NATIONALISM Anthony D. Smith once wrote that the historical imaginary of certain nations has been beaten into common shape "by the hammer of incessant wars."[1] Prolonged warfare especially, he writes, provides the motive force for narratives and images that bolster a sense of cohesion and commonality, that stamp into lasting form a particular storyline of nation. From a certain perspective, the United States of the twenty-first century would appear to qualify as a nation whose self-image has been molded by war, a self-image renewed and reinforced in the current period not only by the wars in Afghanistan and Iraq, but also by a steady drumbeat of imagined and sometimes real threats promoted and amplified in various media—borders under siege, urban uprisings, armed militias, and shadowy agitators fomenting violence. The imagery of war and military ritual, moreover, has penetrated U.S. popular culture to an unprecedented degree, defining what might be called the mentalité of the period—a twenty-first-century warfare theme visible at political rallies and protests, sports events, commemorative flyovers, reenactments, and in the popularity of certain types of video games, paintball, street fashion, and even MREs (Meals Ready-to-Eat) among certain "prepper" populations. A heightened cultural investment in the iconography, imagery, and rhetoric of war has permeated post-9/11 national culture.

The narratives of social cohesion that incessant conflict supposedly supplies, however, are increasingly few. What Jacques Rancière once admiringly called "the dominant fiction" of the United States, the fiction of the "birth of a nation" founded on both external and internecine struggle—an image of social consensus within which members of society are asked to identify themselves—has been refashioned into an image of nation in which a sense of permanent threat and division reigns.[2] Where Smith and Rancière saw a heightened, clarified storyline of nation, immediately recognizable to all, in the narratives that compose national identity, the dominant fiction of the United States has been transformed into a site of struggle in its own right, with competing historical narratives of nation at the center of protest and confrontation.

The contemporary U.S. war film, I argue, brings the antagonistic scripts of national life in the twenty-first century into heightened relief. One of the key genres of the dominant fiction as described by Rancière, the war film has served both as a crystallized expression of a narrative of power, founded on longstanding scenarios and imaginings, as well as the definitive genre of radical contestation. Its shaping of storylines has, at different times, served the ideological purposes of an imperialistic, hegemonic state, while at other times providing a counternarrative of protest and indictment. In the present period, however, narratives of war—mostly centered on omnipresent and elusive threats of terror and counterterror—unfold in an atmosphere of heightened fear and ontological uncertainty, where the combatants are mostly invisible and the codes and conventions of war, as it was once understood, appear to be relics of an older era. The American cinema, Rancière wrote, makes the same film over and over again, forging new iterations on the theme of "the legend of the formation of the code."[3] The contemporary war film, in contrast, pictures the cataclysmic collapse of the code and the emergence of a new set of themes, settings, and dramatis personae.

The films I treat in this study convey a particularly concentrated expression of this changing field of national imaginings. While carrying the deep imprint of the historical past and its shaping ideologies, the six films I consider here depict a world of conflict that can no longer be mapped according to the genre conventions of the past. One of the most dramatic changes I have discovered is the way the core story structures of many foundational U.S. narratives of war—the narrative of rescue, the story of heroic sacrifice, the drama of the mystic brotherhood found only on the battlefield, the ordeal of citizen–soldiers trying to earn their way home—have been reduced to residual expressions, emptied of their original content and replaced with something else. The fading resonance of traditional genre codes also pertains, moreover, to the unifying counterthemes of the anti-war film, where war is pictured as traumatic and degenerate, the wasting of minds and bodies. In my view, neither the traditional codes of war representation nor the equally strong forms of the anti-war film speak to the contemporary historical moment, in which the old grammars of collective violence and resistance to violence have been changed into forms that have not yet been named or described.

In a recent study, film scholar Jonna Eagle argues that the post-9/11 period has been marked by a powerful recuperation of an older cultural paradigm of imperialism and affect, where themes of vulnerability and victimization give rise to compensatory forms of violent agency and fantasies of omnipotence. In political rhetoric and in many popular forms of cultural expression, the wounded national body of the United States in the post-9/11 period has been evoked as justification for an aggressive, violent national response, which carries with it an aura of virtue and righteousness. An older, essentially melodramatic cultural orientation, oscillating between pathos and violent action, provided a familiar paradigm that acquired new relevance after 9/11—the nation as both victimized and invincible. This approach had been articulated and conventionalized throughout the twentieth century in popular genres, such as the Western and the action film. As Eagle writes, "Injury and suffering are linked to the mobilization of violent agency, soliciting identification with a national subject who is constituted as at once vulnerable and powerful."[4]

There is much to consider in Eagle's perceptive diagnosis of the rhetoric of victimization and violence in American national culture, but what I would like to underscore, at least initially, is the emphasis she places on genre as a drive belt connecting the history of society and the history of aesthetic form. As I have argued elsewhere, genres serve as organs of memory for culture, retaining the imprint of the historical period from which they emerged, and carrying with them the layered record of their changing uses.[5] They "remember the past" and make their potentials available for the present.[6] As a genre that rose to prominence in 1898—almost at the beginnings of the cinema—the U.S. war film provides an especially vivid example of genre memory, preserving in its forms and conventions the mediated memory of collective, historical events that have largely shaped the twentieth century. Carried forward from one decade to another, continuously re-inflected with changing generational perspectives and themes, the war film can be seen as a repository of aesthetic ideas concerning power, violence, trauma, honor, and death, a layered record that imbues these films with dense historical capacity. The past seems to circulate in the conventions of the form, acquiring new meanings with each iteration.

In the contemporary moment, however, a deep, fundamental alteration of codes and conventions can be discerned, a transformation of syntax and semantic meanings that is both manifest and subtle. The tectonic shifts now visible in the war film, I argue, expose changes in social reality itself. As the Russian Formalist theorist Pavel Medvedev has written, "Genre appraises reality and reality clarifies genre."[7]

In this volume, I examine several films that explore the changing faces of war and violence in the contemporary period, and that challenge the symbolic framework that representations of war have assumed to date. The films I consider illuminate forms and cultures of warfare that resist the aesthetic patterning to which we have become accustomed. Nowhere in these twenty-first-century works do we find straightforward expression of once familiar scripts—the narratives of sacrifice, heroism, or disillusionment that characterize the genre. Moreover, the forms of violence that these films place in dramatic relief—from the abjection of torture to the procedural violence of the "kill chain," from the hunter–killer paradigm of drone warfare to the visceral terror of the body bomb—cannot be readily accommodated in the frames of symbolic expression provided by an older, twentieth-century war cinema.

The symbolic meaning of violence—its justification or repudiation—is a question that runs like a main current through the genre. In these works, this question is reimagined in a way that touches on what is perhaps the most charged topic in war representation. Although the critical literature on this subject is too vast to summarize here, one of the insights I have found most compelling is Eagle's theme of violent agency as a response to a feeling of national victimization, a theme that she finds in a number of film genres that exploit the affective power of what she calls "sensational melodrama." Spectacular, retributive violence can be scripted as a form of agency, she writes, and further, as a symbolic act of national renewal. This paradigm can be extended in a number of directions. For the literary historian Sarah Cole, for example, violence shapes aesthetic form in fundamental ways. Writing about the effects of World War I on Modernist literature, she distinguishes between what she calls works of enchanted violence, where the violence of war is transmuted through metaphor into an emblem of organic regeneration and renewal, and disenchanted violence, where war's violence is depicted as flat and empty, without symbolic value whatsoever. Most literary works of this period employ a combination of these two modes in representing violence in war. What is not possible, however, is to ignore it. As she writes, "Art neither flees violence, nor transcends it, nor merely represents it, but rather trades on its power."[8] Violence in war has also been represented as an experience of revelation. In the work of Yuval Noah Harari, battlefield experience, what he calls "flesh witnessing," is conceived as the shedding of illusions and the baring of the truth of the self and the world, a subject I will return to below.[9] More recently, an intriguing reading of the World War II combat film defines the spectacular violence of mass combat as an expression of the "destructive sublime."[10]

The violence depicted in films such as *Zero Dark Thirty* (2012), *Eye in the Sky* (2015), and *American Sniper* (2014), however, cannot be readily mapped onto any of these symbolic topoi. In these films, war's violence is presented with extraordinary vividness and gravity, but the larger message it communicates is difficult to pin down. It serves neither as the sanguinary spectacle of redemption that powers many traditional war films, nor as an indictment of war's utter destructiveness and waste. Most surprisingly, the bitter violence of war in these films is depicted chiefly through the experience of the other—the enemy combatant under torture, the last moments of an unwilling suicide bomber, the innocent child caught in the "kill box" of a drone attack. The depiction of violence here is all the more disturbing in that it seems to be absorbed by the Western protagonists of these films almost as their own experience—a mirroring transfer of affect in which the signs of pathos, of visible suffering and loss, are shifted from the victims of the action to the agents. This complicated shift of affect alters the symbolic framework of the war narrative.

And it is here that I see the beginning outlines of a theme resisting the argument for violence as empowering agency, as a righteous response to vulnerability, which clearly animates many earlier war films. Where wounding and victimization once provided the springboard for symbolic displays of punitive and spectacular retribution in the genre films astutely considered by Eagle, the films I treat in this study pointedly undercut the gestures of triumphalism and omnipotence that inhere in much war representation. Although the emotion of vulnerability and the perception of victimization are threaded through these works in complex ways, the symbolic value of violent retribution and the celebration of force as national virtue is suspended. In some cases, the sensationalized violence of the war film genre is criticized, even while it is employed, conveying a kind of complicitous critique, to borrow a phrase from Linda Hutcheon.[11] While stopping short of an explicit anti-war stance, several of the works I treat in this study, including *Zero Dark Thirty* and *American Sniper,* conclude with sober reflections on the costs of violence as a reflex response to a sense of vulnerability. The well-rehearsed genre discourses of war cinema, oscillating between pathos and violent agency, may still inhere in the plot structures of these works, but their symbolic power has been etiolated, drained of any signifying reach.

The power of violence as an aesthetic device, of course, is manifest throughout the history of the genre; the mass choreography of the assault, the shadowy terror of the night patrol, the gruesome intensity of man-to-man fighting, are fulsomely represented in most war films. In my view, however, the narrative and thematic character of violence has shifted in contemporary films, illustrated by the surprising transfer of affect and pathos described above. As a way of mapping the contours of this change, I here briefly summarize one important study of the ways violence has been represented in narratives of war, and the symbolic value it has acquired. Harari argues that war representation underwent an especially revealing transformation with the rise of what he calls flesh witnessing in soldier memoires, a shift that elevated the somatic experience of violence in combat into the singular locus of authenticity and truth.[12]

Sensory experience, he writes, became increasingly valued as a mode of knowledge and privileged insight during the Napoleonic Wars. In earlier periods, soldier narratives of war focused strictly on deeds and events, on the honorary and instrumental actions of combat. In the Romantic period, however, with its growing trust in the senses and the expanding importance assigned to individual experience, warfare began to be understood through a different lens. The senses were now seen as a source of knowledge and even of revelation, and the experience of violence in war was conceived as providing access to a privileged truth about the soldier, war, and the world.

Harari's idea of war's violence as revelation—flesh witnessing as the ultimate truth—provides a powerful description of the classic combat film and its more modern variants, with their characteristic focus on states of heightened psychological and emotional experience amid physical struggle. A film such as *Apocalypse Now* (1979), for example, with its sinister epiphanies, or the grim moments of truth in *Full Metal Jacket* (1987) and *Platoon* (1986), or the existential turning points of films such as *Saving Private Ryan* (1998) and *Courage under Fire* (1996), are shaped around scenes of illumination—war as a kind of Dantean bildung. The films I consider here, however, speak to a different understanding. It is difficult to read the violence of *Zero Dark Thirty*, *The Hurt Locker* (2008), or *Eye in the Sky* in terms of revelation of ultimate truth—a scheme that pervades the imaginative frames of twentieth-century war narratives. Instead, the violence of war is threaded onto an emerging cultural script for conflict—and character—that would be unrecognizable in the narrative worlds of the past. In the drone warfare depicted in *Eye in the Sky*, for example, the targeted violence of the drone strike comes to represent, in the logic of the film, a perverse synthesis of killing and saving, destroying and protecting. And in *Zero Dark Thirty*, for another example, the climactic killing of Osama bin Laden is presented not as a triumphal victory over the ultimate terrorist but as a kind of exorcism, a deed shrouded in night and shadow, screened from the camera's view—an attempt, perhaps, to deny bin Laden a place in the film's larger symbolic order. The strange, unfamiliar patterns of meaning that violence assumes in the war films of the twenty-first century has proven to be one of the most challenging questions I have undertaken in this study.

As I argue in this book, two distinct cultural imaginaries have formed around the subject of contemporary war: one centered on advanced weaponry, remote targeting, and "bodiless" practices of war; the other shaped by the mystique of combat as the ultimate embodied encounter. The films in this study appear to be split between these dramatically different paradigms. In certain works, such as *Zero Dark Thirty* and *Eye in the Sky*, extended sequences detail the gathering and shaping of data into operational vectors of attack, powerfully capturing both the allure and the costs of networked war. In others, such as *The Hurt Locker*, *Restrepo* (2010), and *American Sniper*, the visceral, sensory experience of combat registers as the core subject of the work, providing a close-up view of what the critical geographer Derek Gregory calls the "corpography" of war—a form of sensory awareness, an embodied knowledge of space, terrain, and potential threat that exceeds the disciplines of traditional military planning and intelligence: "By 'corpography' I mean a mode of apprehending, ordering and knowing the battle space through the body as an acutely physical field."[13] These distinct styles of war representation—one defined by technocratic proceduralism, the other by the paradigm of war as extreme corporeal risk—speak to a dichotomy at the heart of the question of how war is imagined today. On the one hand, a fascination with overarching networks of electronic surveillance and sophisticated signals analysis—the prosecution of war at a distance—permeates military theory and planning, expressed in the current enthusiasm for drone warfare, with its illusion of precision. On the other, the imaginative primacy of physical, sensory engagement in combat, where the body at risk takes center stage, has taken hold in many precincts of contemporary life, from combat simulations to the popularity—and almost mythic reputation—of elite combat units such as the Navy SEALs and Delta Force.

Several writers, including Garrett Stewart and Patricia Pisters, have detailed the increasing dominance of the apparatuses of technological war in the narrative representation of combat. Stewart has complained of a diminishing narrative traction in these films, where the great set pieces of war cinema—the mass assault, the stealth incursion into hostile territory, the individual acts of self-sacrifice—seem to have disappeared. What has replaced the traditional dramatic patterning of war cinema, in Stewart's view, is a kind of optical war, a "battle of the screens," lacking force or urgency. In film after film of the early 2000s, he writes, a sense of "digital fatigue" has eroded the energy of the genre.[14] The digital turn in the filmic representation of war that Stewart decries, however, can be seen in a different way, as an aftereffect, an echo of a shift in practical war theory and strategy in the late 1990s, a shift that has come to be enshrined in the phrase "the revolution in military affairs." In the context of war planning and conflict theory, the superiority of virtual, networked war has attained almost doctrinal status. Strategies for wars conducted almost entirely with remote weaponry have, in turn, given rise to a seductive—and deceptive—neologism, "postheroic war," where the soldiers of the dominant power wage war strictly from a distance, far removed from the battle space and actual physical jeopardy. In this paradigm, war has become largely virtual, without risk and without consequence, at least for the soldiers wielding these weapons—virtual war reimagined as "virtuous" war.[15] Where Stewart discerns a shift in film genre codes, the concept of war as virtual—and postheroic—has achieved wide acceptance in military planning.

Nevertheless, a countercurrent can be discerned in the heightened visceral realism of many scenes in the films I treat in this study, sequences that emphasize corporeal experience in a way that comes to feel like a dramatic reassertion of the core principle of war representation—the recuperation of somatic violence into some kind of meaningful frame. In several scenes in these works, tactile images predominate—the stickiness of blood, the pain and panic of torture, the concussion of a roadside bomb—underscoring the power of somatic experience depicted in film and its status as the irreducible subject matter of war cinema. Here too, however, a marked change can be discerned. Not only have the expressive, symbolic dimensions of violence in the war film been reimagined, but the protagonists of the combat narrative have changed as well, in fundamental ways. The major players in *The Hurt Locker, A Private War* (2018), *Zero Dark Thirty,* and *American Sniper* all exhibit a common and surprising trait. Exceptionally skillful, gifted in their tradecraft and fieldwork, they are driven by what Thomas Elsaesser calls a condition of "productive pathology"—an ability to perform that is helped rather than hindered by pathological tendencies. What would ordinarily be seen as self-destructive and lethally dangerous behavior, where compulsion, obsessiveness, and an attraction to extreme danger places others at risk along with the protagonist, becomes a key to the character's success—and a necessary tool of survival. Nowhere in the war films of the past do we find similar protagonists, characters who continuously push themselves to the edge, as Sergeant William James (Jeremy Renner) in *The Hurt Locker* and Marie Colvin (Rosamund Pike) in *A Private War* repeatedly do. In these figures, the styles of behavior once reserved in films of war for the soldier who has "crossed the line" into suicidal recklessness are here treated, with minor differences, as essential to the arc of the narrative.

Another striking change in the war films of the current period is the emergence of female characters as principal agents of the narrative. In three of the six films I treat in this study—*Zero Dark Thirty, Eye in the Sky,* and *A Private War*—women are not only central to the stories, they generate the events of the plot, pushing the narrative forward at each of its defining points. Yvonne Tasker has written of certain earlier depictions of female soldiers, such as we see in the films *GI Jane* (1997) and *Courage under Fire*, as "masculinized," women performing a role that has simply been borrowed, more or less whole cloth, from stereotypical male styles of combat performance.[16] Recent portrayals, however, such as the CIA agent Maya (Jessica Chastain) in *Zero Dark Thirty,* or Colonel Katherine Powell (Helen Mirren) in *Eye in the Sky,* or Marie Colvin in *A Private War,* are far different. For one thing, they are not defined by the bildungsroman formula of so many war films—the emergence of the young man through the experience of violence and loss—a paradigm that informs such well-known works as *Platoon, Born on the Fourth of July* (1989), *Full Metal Jacket,* and *Fury* (2014). The existential education of the young soldier in the grim truths that only battlefield experience reveals is nowhere on the agenda of *Zero Dark Thirty* or *Eye in the Sky.* Rather, the female characters in these films are portrayed in ways that are entirely unfamiliar, providing each film with a protagonist that cannot readily be mapped onto past iterations.

The shifts that I describe here are highlighted by the importance of the filmmaker Kathryn Bigelow in transforming the genre of the war film. The prominence of Bigelow, director of the two works that form the opening chapters of this study, *The Hurt Locker* and *Zero Dark Thirty*, marks a further turn away from the relentlessly masculine gendering of both character and authorship in the genre. While women filmmakers have directed films of war, including Agnieszka Holland with *In Darkness* (2011), Gillian Armstrong with *Charlotte Gray* (2001), and Angelina Jolie with *Unbroken* (2014)—all set in World War II—the visibility of Bigelow as the director of what are arguably the two most celebrated and influential war films of the twenty-first century is noteworthy. Both *The Hurt Locker* and *Zero Dark Thirty* bring an entirely new perspective to the war film genre, exposing and decoding the violence of contemporary war—whose forms and characteristics, I argue, have changed—and featuring protagonists who possess none of the characteristics of the charismatic hero. The violence that initiates and permeates both films, for example, varies dramatically from what we have seen in films before. Here, IEDs, suicide bombers, corpse bombs, and sudden terror attacks are set against the institutionalized torture and high-tech killing administered by American agents. Mortal threat, in the worlds portrayed in *The Hurt Locker* and *Zero Dark Thirty*, is embedded in the daily textures of life in a period of conflict that seems to have no limit. In both films, moreover, the protagonists, William James and Maya are portrayed as solitary, enigmatic, and wholly identified with their war work in a way that precludes any sense of genre familiarity or the possibility of gaining a larger insight into character. Bigelow's work disarms genre expectations and creates a new language of combat violence that will come to have a paramount influence on the way war is imagined and represented in the twenty-first century.

Changes in film genres of this magnitude are generally discovered only retrospectively, as new forms of symbolic expression are shaped not by a singular event but a complex array of social and historical factors. Although the attacks of 9/11 mark a decisive break point in American social and political history—an event that demarcates the "before" of the twentieth century from the "after" of the twenty-first—aesthetic transformations such as I describe occur not as a punctual reaction but rather by way of accretion, as a cultural response to a series of mutations in social life, historical experience, and aesthetic form. A comparison might be drawn to the retrospective construction of film noir, which was earlier called the psychological thriller. The shifts in form and content in what has become one of the most celebrated film genres of the twentieth century were not identified and named until well after many of the classic examples of the form had appeared, including films such as *Double Indemnity* (1944), *Scarlet Street* (1945), and *In a Lonely Place* (1950). And there is still a lively intellectual debate over the relative importance of various cultural, historical, and artistic influences in shaping this now-canonical genre, ranging from the influence of German Expressionism, to postwar trauma, to the displacement of the male subject in the postwar economy, to the popularity of psychoanalysis in the period.

Identifying the historical events and aesthetic changes that have led to the shifts I describe is thus a challenge I approach with caution, although some provisional thoughts and speculations are worth sharing. First, the events of 9/11 precipitated fundamental changes in the broad sense of national identity in the United States—the complex array of myth and history, daily life and social ritual, collective practices and the symbols of belonging, usually underpinned by narrative—that creates a sense of national coherence. Although 9/11 catalyzed an immediate and initially powerful rehearsal of national symbols and signs of collective purpose—the raising of the flag on the ruins of Ground Zero, the twin beams of light emanating from the destruction, and somewhat later George W. Bush's "Mission Accomplished" speech on the deck of an aircraft carrier—symbols and gestures that evoked the iconic imagery of earlier wars—it was clear that something fundamental had changed. The older narrative and symbolic construction of nation—as a gleaming and inviolate city upon a hill, as a land of many peoples forged in a singular union, secure in its territorial boundaries—could no longer capture the new historical reality of sudden mass terror, nor imaginatively assuage the sense of national vulnerability and insecurity that had taken hold.

Moreover, the cynical exploitation of the imagery of threat, visible especially in the escalation of anti-Muslim and anti-immigrant bias, congealed into a competing narrative of nativist belonging. The invisible threads of terror, with its hidden networks and shadowy alliances, seemed, for some, to penetrate the subjective experience of daily life, giving rise to a widespread sense of insecurity and of a nation at risk—a sense of cultural and historical instability that has played out in a wide range of social manifestations. What I describe above as the dominant fiction, the imaginative constructs that give coherence to national life, began to collapse. As concepts of nation began to shift, the genre forms and narratives that buttress a sense of belonging and belief began to change as well, their affective currents began to flow in new and different directions. In particular, the genre of the war film, with its stories of sacrifice, rescue, and brotherhood, and the equally powerful form of the anti-war film, with its scenes of moral reckoning and personal and collective loss, has been converted to the expression of something else.

The stories and themes associated with the traditional war film, however—the great dramatic narratives of collective power marshaled to protect or restore a civilizational order—have not disappeared altogether, but have migrated to the Superhero genre. Here a confederation of heroes, each with different strengths and hailing from different spheres of disparate worlds, lines up against the forces of galactic evil. In the Superhero genre, we find a return to the themes of brotherhood, to the narrative of rescue, to the scene of heroic sacrifice—narrative tropes that can no longer be directly expressed, or that no longer have signifying reach, in a war film genre whose major social and cultural role has shifted.

And here I will offer a second speculation concerning the causes, or at least one of the corollaries, of the changes I discern. In a historical moment when the imagery and rhetoric of war is ascendant on the domestic front, the war film as genre now seems to engage dialogically with contemporary scenes of domestic conflict that have rocked civil society in the United States, conflicts that often carry a violent, warlike accent. The tone and emotional color of these films resonates in some perhaps unspecifiable way with the aggravated tensions that now permeate contemporary political and social life and have resulted in an increasingly divisive experience of nation. The films I treat in this study are dominated by a sense of continuous threat, traumatic loss, and the internal violence that imbues many of the characters' psychic lives. Endless wars without a mission have become the ground and the basic semantic material for heightened dramas of existential risk without resolution or redemption, characteristics that now define ordinary experience in the homeland as well.

More concretely—and here I will set forth a third hypothesis—the peculiar features of war in the twenty-first century place a particular and novel pressure on the conventions of war cinema. The anonymity of the enemy; the geographical remoteness of the wars in Afghanistan and Iraq; the endlessly deferred moments of triumph or defeat in conflicts that have been aptly named the "forever wars"; the repeated and multiple deployments of troops, in a series of "surges" that have little effect; the prosecution of war at a distance, in which the soldier, following a killing mission, resumes a conventional, civilian and suburban life in the evening after work; the invisibility of both the agents and the victims of war, as more and more fighting is carried out in drone strikes or in top secret raids conducted by "black ops" soldiers; the blurring of the lines between enlisted soldiers and contractors; the almost complete absence of public awareness, despite the relentless exploitation of soldiers for public relations purposes. If we look to the films themselves, the lingering mood is one of fraught emotional suspension: there is no teleological resolution in these works.

Several films, including *Zero Dark Thirty, The Hurt Locker, A Private War,* and *Eye in the Sky,* conclude with scenes that suggest that war in the twenty-first century is a permanent, ongoing condition, that the cycle of violence continues, that the few moments of charged collective engagement in scenes of traditional martial struggle lead almost nowhere. The wars continue and the soldier fights alone. In many ways, the films of this study push up against the unsayable, refuting ordinary forms of symbolic and imaginative resolution, confounding any kind of mastery through narrative, while at the same time demanding to be seen and heard.

CHAPTER SUMMARIES

In the first chapter, I consider Kathryn Bigelow's Best Picture Award–winning film *The Hurt Locker,* arguing that it serves as both the aesthetic summa and the final curtain of the traditional war film genre. Evoking the major motifs and themes of war cinema, including the rescue narrative and the pathos of individual sacrifice, *The Hurt*

Locker indexes the emotional power the formulas of the past once carried, and then quietly dramatizes their fading resonance for the new wars of the twenty-first century. Sergeant William James, the leader of the bomb disposal squad and the protagonist of the film, embodies both consummate skill and a compulsive attraction to danger. James's flamboyant, almost theatrical performances, his deliberate pursuit of the extreme edge of risk in disarming hidden explosives, evince a heightened vocation for war—like a Navy SEAL or a Delta Force soldier whose rarified skills are designed for combat, and who cannot function effectively in any other setting.

Yet for all its close attention to this uncharted zone of combat experience, *The Hurt Locker* is in many ways a deeply historical text, engaging with the history of war representation in film while at the same time refusing the symbolic solutions, the deep appeal to codes of collective belief that create a "feeling of commonality" as described by film scholar Hermann Kappelhoff. In the gap between the conventions of the past, where embodied violence was often given a redemptive shape, and the unredeemed violence in war films of the twenty-first century, the film finds its dramatic subject and complex mode of address. *The Hurt Locker* recalls older codes and conventions of the war film, summoning them as a form of genre memory, only to sweep them away in new forms of violent encounter.

In chapter 2, I explore the unlikely combination of embodied violence and procedural analysis that takes shape around the hunt for Osama bin Laden in *Zero Dark Thirty.* The expressive violence depicted in the film is both intimate and enacted at a distance, rendered in the haptic assaults of torture, terror, and violent attack that bookend the narrative, and expressed, in the middle section, in the dragnet of surveillance and tracking data constructed to track bin Laden, where each data point, terrorist photograph, and intercepted communication maps a history of violence and a script for potential attack. *Zero Dark Thirty*'s detailed exploration of counterterrorism—including its depiction of torture and rendition, the secret raid on bin Laden's compound, and the umbrella of surveillance that has been superimposed on global life—conveys the present historical moment in all its dark reality, while at the same time opening a space of imaginative projection.

The main character, Maya, provides a critical link among the three sections of the film, a character whose intelligence, willingness to do the dirty work, and implacable resolve form the center of the drama. A new kind of agent of war, Maya conveys an unsettling ambiguity, displaying exceptional skill and focus, with none of the characteristics of the charismatic hero. In a film that has few of the tropes or characteristics conventionally associated with war cinema, its most compelling figure is the character of Maya, who seems to come from a variant genre that has not yet been named.

In chapter 3, I explore the aura of technological and psychological invincibility that has emerged around drone warfare, a weapons system that has radically transformed military tactics in the West and assumed an almost magical potency in the wider life of culture. Looking closely at the dramatic film *Eye in the Sky*, I consider the transformative role of the drone in the conceptual and practical frameworks of war, detailing the way it has overturned traditional models of hostile and friendly territory, lethal force, and even notions of the battlefield itself.

Eye in the Sky centers on the moral, existential, and tactical issues that confront the drone pilots, military commanders, and political and legal staffs—the "kill chain" of drone warfare—as they plan and execute a strike on a terrorist cell in Kenya, a "friendly" country with which the West is not at war. Complicating the tactical, legal, and political calculus that must be considered in authorizing and executing the strike, the members of the kill chain must also consider that an innocent bystander, a young girl named Alia, has wandered into the blast zone just before the launch. The film illustrates how the drone, far from encouraging an abstract, distanced, "bloodless" form of killing as is so often imagined, foregrounds a palpable intimacy with the victim, an almost tactile contact between the victims and the agents of violence.

The story of Marie Colvin, a celebrated American war correspondent who worked for the British *Sunday Times* and was murdered by the Syrian military in 2013, brings several new dimensions of contemporary war into view, as discussed in chapter 4. Colvin's primary focus as a conflict journalist was the deliberate targeting of civilians as a strategy of war. Her heroic commitment to exposing the suffering of women and children in conflict zones throughout the world, however, came with great costs. *A Private War* frames the story of Colvin with two sequences in which she is attacked by soldiers: opening with a scene of a grenade attack that costs her the vision in her left eye, and concluding with the missile attack in Homs, Syria, which cost her her life.

In its portrayal of Colvin, the film explores both the subjectivity of the main character—driven by ambition and plagued by traumatic memory—as well as the shifting frames of war in twenty-first-century conflict, where stories of atrocity reported by war journalists are perceived as a direct threat to powerful regimes. Colvin as protagonist represents a new turn in the cinematic representation of combat and a new figuration of the war correspondent—a woman whose talent and courage carry a self-destructive charge, whose drive for direct, visceral experience become an addiction—another example of the productive pathology that distinguishes the lead characters of many of the films in this study.

Chapter 5 examines how four documentary projects produced by photographer Tim Hetherington and the writer Sebastian Junger in Afghanistan raise several challenging issues of war representation. Embedded for over a year with soldiers from Battle Company, an army detachment in a remote outpost in the Korengal Valley, Hetherington and Junger's work brings into view critical concerns about the role and objectivity of embedded journalists in war. Some writers have faulted *Restrepo,* for example, for not being sufficiently critical, for being partial to the soldiers, perhaps even complicit with acts of violence in war, with one calling it a "paramilitary film."[17] I argue that the film, far from endorsing war, conveys a complex and subtle critique. Evoking the cultural history embedded in genre, the film can be seen as an example of double voicing, as it calls up the memory of past war representations to open a channel to a deeper reading of the text.

The photographs collected in the large photo book *Infidel* by Hetherington and Junger, in contrast, depict the soldiers of Battle Company engaged in the quotidian activities of life in the outpost, punctuated by scenes of the men on patrol and in combat. In many of these images, the soldiers are depicted performing what Kristen Whissel calls the masculine "rhetoric of soldiery"—working out, wielding weapons and carrying ammunition, comparing tattoos, wrestling, and sometimes displaying open affection for one another.[18] Other photographic images—such as the shot of the exhausted, perhaps traumatized soldier Brandon Olson, the World Press Photo Award winner in 2008—communicate a very different message, conveying isolation, psychological injury, and dread.

The short photo essay by Hetherington, *Into the Korengal*, published in 2011, departs from the almost exclusive focus on American troops that defines the main body of Hetherington and Junger's work in the Korengal, focusing on Afghan males, of different ages, interacting with the soldiers of Battle Company. Although the photo essay is short—it contains only eight images, accompanied by Hetherington's written commentary—it is instructive, suggesting an incipient counternarrative to the one-sided depictions in Western media. It shows Afghan men engaging with and reacting to U.S. soldiers in a way that reveals something of the emotional dynamics of occupation. These images of Afghan males, as infrequent as they are, serve as counterpoint to the Western stereotype of Afghanistan masculinity as "belligerent, dead, or absent," in the words of the photography scholar Saumava Mitra.[19]

The short video that Hetherington released at roughly the same time as *Restrepo, Sleeping Soldiers—single screen* (2009), serves as a complement and accompaniment to the feature-length film, bringing different themes to light. Originating as a series of still photographs of the soldiers of Battle Company sleeping in the small mountain redoubt nicknamed OP Restrepo, Hetherington superimposed live-action scenes and recorded sounds and voices on still shots to create a short film that is associative, dreamlike, and haunted. In the video, the faces of the soldiers are unmarked and youthful. Layered over their sleeping faces, however, are the sounds and images of battle and the voices of colleagues in distress, suggesting the penetration of violence into the deep fabric of psychic life.

In chapter 6, I argue that *American Sniper* performs an immanent critique of war and the culture of violence that pervades American life, while embedding its critical perspective in a form that gives full credence to the commitment and sense of purpose of ordinary soldiers. In its use of genre conventions, the film employs a complex double voice: the spectacle and drama of combat is rendered in a familiar cinematic language of kinetic intensity and then reframed, through patterns of doubling and reversal, to reveal the psychic and social costs of war's violence, which in the words of one character "consumes one completely." The film presents a complex dramatization of PTSD and moral injury. The feral violence of war, which is rendered with gruesome intensity in the scenes set in Iraq, penetrates the psychic life of the character Chris Kyle, the legendary sniper of the film's title, who returns, again and again, for multiple deployments in Iraq. On his returns home, however, between deployments, the psychological toll manifests itself. As Kyle's psychic stability degenerates, the extreme violence of the Iraq War—the violence he witnesses and the violence he metes out—follows him into the domestic spaces of his suburban home. Brooding, unresponsive, subject to hallucinations, the character becomes a danger to himself and his family.

The film explores the dark underside of one of the most foundational enabling myths of American culture, the strand of the dominant fiction that celebrates violent agency as a way of protecting the vulnerable and preserving the institutions of American life. In the film's depiction of the character of Chris Kyle, the costs of endless war are represented in a way that speaks to a larger contemporary social reality, where the combat soldier returns, often damaged and unstable, not to a diurnal homeland of pastoral beauty, but to a shadow world filled with imagined threats and permeated by guilt.

The films I consider in this volume play a critical role in bringing into focus the way war is imagined and represented in the twenty-first century, where ingrained patterns of expression and meaning—the narrative structures that have underpinned representations of war for well over a century—have been emphatically altered. Each chapter examines a different aspect of the evolving face of war representation, changes that reflect a shift not only in the aesthetics of genre but in military practices, social behaviors, and what is considered acceptable as a cost of war. The power of cinema to illuminate the historical continuities and changes in the national imaginary that the war film brings into relief provides the impetus for this book.

CHAPTER 1

EMBODIMENT AND PATHOS IN THE WAR FILM

The Hurt Locker

BEGINNING WITH AN EPIGRAPH from the author Chris Hedges—"The rush of battle is often a potent and lethal addiction, for war is a drug"—*The Hurt Locker* (2008) immediately conveys a picture of war that would have been unimaginable in the war films of the twentieth century.[1] Framing combat as an addictive pleasure, an ongoing private and collective need, the film departs radically from genre convention, evoking and then abandoning the familiar formulas of sacrifice and loss that have structured the genre from its inception in favor of a mode of address that emphasizes the adrenalized experience of risk. Although the allure of extreme physical risk appears as a motif in several earlier war films, including *The Deer Hunter* (1978) and *Apocalypse Now* (1979), *The Hurt Locker* explores this idea as its primary theme, relocating the central focus of its narrative to a private zone of somatic experience, outside any larger metanarrative of nation or history. Instead, a mood of pure visceral excitement prevails: in the figure of Sergeant William James (Jeremy Renner), the leader of a bomb disposal squad, the anxiety of entering a perilous no-man's-land is matched by the exhilaration of locating the hidden triggers, finding the secret connections, living life in a threshold state where discovery and revelation are instantly counterpointed by the threat of annihilation. Foregrounding the almost erotic charge of defusing hidden bombs, the film underlines the "meaning" that war gives as a form of intense bodily excitement, personalized, in which the palpable experience of the body at risk is separated from any larger justification or narrative of purpose.

The Hurt Locker centers on a small team of three U.S. soldiers during the war in Iraq, assigned to a bomb disposal or EOD (Explosive Ordnance Disposal) unit, attempting to complete safely their mission in the waning days of their posting. The film begins in medias res, commencing in the middle of an operation in a busy Baghdad market. Led by Sergeant Matt Thompson (Guy Pearce), the team is shown attempting to detonate a large IED that has been spotted amid some trash. The team emanates a sense of confident and focused ability, and Thompson appears to be competent, well-liked, and protective of his men. While attempting to detonate the explosive, however, Thompson is killed in action.

With this early combat death shadowing the action, the plotting of the film takes a number of surprising turns. Thompson's replacement as team leader, James, has a maverick sensibility that pulls the narrative into unfamiliar scenarios. He brings to the job a unique approach and a unique set of skills. Rather than emphasizing the safety of his men, he is attracted to danger; rather than functioning as leader of the team, he ignores his two colleagues' urgent warnings and tries to work alone, amplifying the risk they take with every assignment. He pushes the limits of his own skill and compromises the lives of his men in a compulsive drive to master whatever challenge he encounters, from figuring out the complex wiring of a car laden with explosives, to disabling and removing a bomb sewn into the corpse of a young boy, to attempting to release a suicide bomber from his explosive vest. The other two team members, Sergeant J. T. Sanborn (Anthony Mackie), and Specialist Owen Eldridge (Brian Geraghty), press James to follow protocol, to detonate rather than disable the IEDs when possible, to use the robot vehicle to deliver the charge to detonate the bomb, to wear the Kevlar bomb suit. James, however, persists in carrying out his work in the most dangerous way he can devise. His team members, whose hazardous job has suddenly become even more fraught, consider setting off an explosion that will "accidentally" kill him. In a series of encounters that become increasingly perilous, James's intricate and daring performances of skill and initiative are set against his team's conviction that he will cost them their lives. Under James's command, their remaining days of deployment have become searing, high-wire dramas.

Thomas Elsaesser has described the film's central character, Sergeant James, as a figure whose exceptional skills are enhanced by an extreme psychological orientation, a combination that he calls "productive pathology."[2] In four set pieces that form the armature of the film, James seems to cultivate lethal risk, defusing bombs with a minimum of equipment or armor, and persisting in the task well beyond any pragmatic justification. James's flamboyant, theatrical performances, his deliberate pursuit of what one writer calls the "edgework" of the modern soldier, evince a heightened vocation for war, like a special ops soldier—a Navy SEAL or a Delta Force operative—whose rarified skills are designed for combat and who cannot exist without it.[3] With its close attention to this previously uncharted zone of extreme combat experience, the film opens a new chapter in the representation of war.

OVERTURE

Set during the second year of the Iraq War, the film depicts a Baghdad pocked with menace. Bombs concealed in piles of trash and in abandoned cars, explosives buried only inches deep in the dirt of apartment courtyards and sewn into corpses, snipers perched on balconies—the atlas of threats depicted in the film gives the city a remarkably sinister aspect, with every shopkeeper and passerby a potential source of harm. Ordinary conversations turn out to be setups for imminent aggression. In addition, the visibility of the team's operations puts them under the constant gaze of the local population, exposing them to continuous surveillance from apartment balconies, the street, and the minarets. Unlike the conventional war film, with its ebb and flow of struggle, its scenes of combat chaos interspersed with more tranquil episodes of watchful calm, a condition of unrelieved tension takes hold; *The Hurt Locker* has none of the ordinary rhythms that have shaped the dramatic structure of the war film for over a century.

The film's rethinking of the conventions of genre is crystallized in its opening scene. A ground-level shot from a robot camera introduces the sequence, tracking forward in an uneven, jostling motion accompanied by bursts of radio static, shouted commands through megaphones, the singing of prayers from a mosque, and the urban cacophony of a busy street at midday. Without preamble, *The Hurt Locker* opens on a U.S. military operation being conducted in full daylight, in the middle of a Baghdad market. Multiple shots from different perspectives, composed for maximum contrast and discontinuity, follow the opening robot cam tracking shot—a rapid-fire panoramic montage that introduces us to the social and geographic milieu in which the film will unfold. A perimeter is being established. Concealed within the folds and textures of the urban landscape, a possible IED has been identified in a suspicious pile of trash near a major intersection. As the robot approaches the target—a progress rendered in multiple shots from different angles—a disorienting vision of a Middle Eastern urban center, in the middle of a war, begins to take shape, a kind of weird variant on the famous "city symphony" genre pioneered by Dziga Vertov and Walter Ruttmann. Here, an ancient metropolis and its ingrained rhythms of daily life are crosshatched by the sounds and sights of modern war: shopkeepers hawk their goods as jets scream overhead; vegetable stands and butcher shops conduct business next to the shells of bombed-out cars rusting in the sun; a herd of goats crosses the path of the robot bomb-finder forcing a military operation to pause. The collage of unlikely sights and sounds that open the film places the viewer in a world that is both familiar and strange.

The din and confusion of the opening shots quickly gives way to a scene of relative calm and control. The EOD team directing the robot to its target has set up a provisional command center in a secure space behind their Humvee, where they view the robot's video feed on a monitor in the back of the vehicle, and from where they remotely move the robot into place. The team of three soldiers appears confident, tested, and locked in. They share jokes as they identify the type of bomb they are dealing with, assess the size of the ordnance they have discovered, and decide on a method of detonation. The team, consisting of three men ranging in age and experience—Sergeant Thompson (the team leader), Sergeant Sanborn, and Specialist Eldridge—are a typical war cinema assemblage of disparate characters, recognizable from previous iterations of combat films. Sergeant Thompson, in particular, arrives on-screen as a figure familiar from the long history of the genre. A paragon of homosocial masculinity, Thompson's speech and figure behavior bring into view a constellation of Hollywood hero characteristics: handsome, at ease with his men, he deflects fear and anxiety by bantering with his young team while simultaneously making an expert evaluation of the blast radius and the procedures they will follow. In the first minutes of the film, we are introduced to a character that would ordinarily be at the center of the story and wear the hero's mantle.

When the initial plan to detonate the bomb breaks down, however, Thompson must don a heavy Kevlar bomb suit and physically carry the detonating explosives to the hidden device. A nervous stasis takes hold, as the team's range of motion is circumscribed by the requirements of the mission. In contrast to the rapid pace of the editing and the speeded-up pans and zooms of the camera, the ponderous, dreamlike movements of Thompson, encased in his bomb suit, impose a counterrhythm on the scene. Clothed in high-tech armor, wired for radio communication, Thompson enters the kill zone with slowed, careful movements, carrying the charge that he will use to detonate the IED. As he lays the explosive charge on the bomb, the two other team members tasked with surveilling the area for threats transmit their apprehension through their microphones, communicating a sense of high tension. After planting the charge, Thompson begins the long walk back to the armored vehicle.

One writer has described war as an "embodied medium of imagination and experience," an idea that is powerfully expressed throughout *The Hurt Locker* and is especially visible in the opening segment.[4] In the film's initial bomb disposal scene, sense impressions dominate—the amplified heartbeat, the quickened breathing, the labor of motion—conveying a physical, phenomenological experience of bodily risk that is unmatched in contemporary cinema. Along with the acoustic layering of the sounds of the city and the microphone communications of the soldiers, the optics of multiple cameras translate the kinesthetic impressions of a combat operation into a somatic drama.

As the scene progresses, the expressive contrasts of tempo and movement that have dominated the film so far build to a crescendo. With Thompson still in the kill zone, Eldridge, the youngest team member, spots a potential triggerman in the marketplace. Ordered by Sanborn to "burn" the possible assassin—a man holding a cell phone—Eldridge cannot get a shot and then cannot pull the trigger.

The death of Thompson. *The Hurt Locker,* directed by Kathryn Bigelow, 2008. Produced by Kathryn Bigelow, Mark Boal, Nicolas Chartier, and Greg Shapiro.

Sanborn continues to shout at Eldridge to shoot the man. Hearing the commotion through the speaker in his helmet, Thompson begins to run: slowed by the armor, it is as if he were running underwater. His accelerated heartbeat, his labored breathing, the shouts into the microphones—the close-up sound design and rapid-fire editing convey a sense of near panic. Running toward the protection of the armored vehicle, unable to move fast enough to escape the blast, Thompson's suit becomes his coffin, a high-tech carapace not strong enough to protect him from the shock of the blast but too heavy to allow him to escape.

In the alternation of slow-motion and naturalistic tempo in the rendering of Thompson's death—an event portrayed from several angles and speeds—we are reminded that the war film is fundamentally a machine for making emotions. With the body of the team leader falling nearly into the space of the spectator, the inside of his visor smeared with blood, the scene's affective power is placed in relief. Thompson is driven toward the camera by the explosion, arms outstretched, his death conveying a powerful visual message of loss, a message that is reinforced by the genre memory of countless battlefield films, photos, and paintings. Placed before our gaze and held there, in a near freeze frame of ten seconds' duration, the body of the soldier is depicted in a way that insists that death be recognized.

GENRE MEMORY / EXPRESSIVE MOVEMENT / PATHOS

The death of Thompson, in my view, marks both the aesthetic summa as well as the final curtain of the twentieth-century war film. The scene's sustained kinetic drama, followed by an image of pathos that is as powerful as any in the cinema of war, both summarizes and reframes a century-long tradition of combat representation in film, distilled here into its fundamental components. In its formal patterning—a virtuoso orchestration of affect around staccato contrasts of movement and stillness, close-up and long shot, repetition and progress—the scene recalls the complex montage arpeggios of Sergei Eisenstein's *October* (1928) and *Battleship Potemkin* (1925). And in the sudden, harrowing transition from dynamic movement to the near stasis that follows the explosion, the film underlines the power of violence as an aesthetic device, highlighting the close connection between violence and aesthetic form that the war film exemplifies and confirms.

The long pictorial tradition of violent death in battle, familiar from films, photographs, paintings, and other art forms, is evoked in this sequence. As the literary theorists Gary Saul Morson and Caryl Emerson write, genres "remember the past, and make their resources available for the present."[5] Indeed, in the low-angle framing of Thompson's body, the dramatic foreshortening of his figure, and the visual softening of the background, the film rehearses some of the earliest techniques of war photography, designed to accentuate the pathos of death on the battlefield.

And yet the violence of Thompson's death signals, with equal force, a departure from the past. Its powerful imagery of pathos, a key feature of war representation, occurs as if in a vacuum, outside any larger historical or cultural metanarrative. The violence of death in battle, and the emotion it invariably generates, is here detached from any recognizable theme; its function as a symbol standing in for something larger seems to be annulled. The sequence disturbs the traditional codes of war cinema, isolating the sacrifice of the soldier from any larger questions of nation or history. In a contemporary period defined by endless, permanent war, where any sense of historical dimension or social consequence has been erased, the death of the soldier is framed not by a "sense of commonality," as Hermann Kappelhoff has described it, but by a symbolic void.[6] Thompson's killing is no longer readable as sacrifice for nation, or as its opposite, victimization and waste; its pathos carries neither a wider social sanction nor a sense of anti-war conviction. It has relinquished its symbolic authority: the film refuses to track the death of Thompson into an overarching cultural script. In this extraordinary opening sequence, in which no rifles are fired, no hand-to-hand struggle occurs, and no enemy is clearly identified, the meaning of violence in war has changed.

As Kappelhoff has argued, the Hollywood war film revolves around the construction of a sense of commonality, a feeling of community. And the core mechanism for generating a sense of community is the scene of the young soldier's sacrifice and the pathos that surrounds it. In the blinding moment of transition from life to death, in the almost instantaneous passage from one state to another, Kappelhoff writes, the fundamental dramatic conflict of the Hollywood war film is crystallized, "the difference between the meaningful death of the sacrifice for and the meaningless death of the individual through the actions of the nation, the difference between sacrifice and victim."[7] In scenes of combat sacrifice, the death of the soldier is charged with a higher meaning, usually tied to an ideal of nation. The sacrificial death becomes a heroic death, often by linking death or burial with the idea of community renewal.[8] Conversely, anti-war films that reject the notion of nation or the military as a form of "higher meaning" also evoke a sense of commonality, as the pathos aroused in these films is effectively converted into a collective revulsion toward war.

Although the archetypes and combat scenarios of sacrifice and pathos that define the long history of the genre are present in the scene, they are evoked mainly as a shadow text, summoned to highlight the radical differences in the features and character of contemporary war. In the scene's culminating moment of violence and loss, the usual interpretive conventions fall away. And in the short, sad scene that follows the death of Thompson, as Sanborn says farewell to his team leader—silent and alone in a neon-lit room containing the boxes of several soldiers' personal effects—a sense of diminishment takes hold. The mourning scene—a trope that had once brought with it a heightened affective charge, a sense of catharsis—is pictured as small in scale, reduced almost to nothing. At this point we might take as our cue the film's enigmatic title. The hurt and anguish of war is evoked and at the same time suppressed, aroused but refused any symbolic resolution, called forth but detached from any communal system of meaning. Both rehearsing and departing from genre convention, the opening scene of *The Hurt Locker* can be understood as the first move in an ongoing cinematic engagement with the radically different contours of contemporary war.

PRODUCTIVE PATHOLOGIES

Also missing from *The Hurt Locker* are the spectacular and harrowing combat scenes of earlier periods—the night patrol, the stealth incursion behind enemy lines, the bombardment and assault, the mass choreography of battle and the gruesome intensity of individual combat. The violence the film explores has a very different character, conveying an almost anthropological interest in risk and vulnerability. Emphasizing the intricate, dangerous work of the EOD team, the film explores the edgework of the modern soldier, the threshold states of physical risk, as if the depiction of extreme states might provide an opening to a new imagining of war.

Sergeant James, the new leader of the EOD team following Thompson's death, enters the film almost as a mutant life-form—solitary, intoxicated with adrenalin, and consummately skillful. His first encounter with Sanborn, his new team member, is marked by James's antisocial gestures—turning his metal music up loudly when he decides he is done with the conversation, and tearing the protective sheeting off the windows of their shared hooch despite Sanborn's protestations. Elsaesser writes that the film provides us with a strong example of the male productive pathology hero: "Sgt. William James . . . is considered reckless and unpredictable in his behavior, to the point that one member of his unit is ready to kill him, by deliberately triggering an explosion. But James turns out to be superbly attuned to his specialized job . . . it is in the extreme war situation that [his] maladjustment turns out to be an advantage."[9] In the asymmetric, technological wars of the present, which combine features of distanced war with the close at hand engagements of guerilla war, civil war, and wars of occupation, a new kind of "distributed subjectivity" is required—in Elsaesser's view, a subjectivity that can improvise, that can function well in conditions of "data overload," a productive pathology that may point to "our survival skills as a species."[10]

His reading of the protagonist of *The Hurt Locker* has the singular merit of describing a new type of character for what I argue is a new set of genre coordinates. Although his analysis ranges broadly over Hollywood genre films, I feel the model of productive pathology is particularly useful for helping us come to grips with the peculiarities of Sergeant James and several other of the protagonists of the films I consider in this book. The protagonist of *The Hurt Locker,* in particular, seems utterly unlike the figures we know from previous war films, including the character with whom he is most often compared—Captain Benjamin L. Willard (Martin Sheen) in *Apocalypse Now.*[11] Indeed, the differences between these two iconic figures of the modern war film are far more pronounced than their similarities. Captain Willard, ordered to assassinate the renegade American colonel Walter E. Kurtz (Marlon Brando), is mainly an observer of the action, watching and commenting as the events of the plot unfold, frequently narrating his thoughts and reactions in voice-over. Throughout most of the film, he is acted upon; he is not the agent of the narrative. As Colonel Kurtz says, near the climax of the film, he is neither a soldier nor an assassin; he is a "grocery clerk come to collect the bill." The protagonist of *Apocalypse Now,* for all his dark anomie, can be seen as a variant of a familiar form of split protagonist, caught in an internal conflict between darkness and light—a struggle, as General R. Corman (G. D. Spradlin) at the beginning of the film puts it, between destructive impulses and "the better angels of our nature."

For Sergeant James, by contrast, the meaning of war is in the improvised actions he performs alone. He is driven by what the author Chris Hedges calls the "lethal addiction" of combat risk, of extreme action rather than reflection. Nowhere in his world is there room for interior monologue, introspection, or existential ruminations of the sort engaged in by Willard. The deep dive into the mirror world that pulls Willard toward his encounter with Kurtz is simply not present in *The Hurt Locker.* Rather, James is defined by the extreme, almost theatrical demands he makes on himself in dismantling bombs ("823 so far," as he tells the commanding officer)—a productive pathology unlike any the genre has heretofore produced. Radical in his approach to his work, James marks an extreme in the portrayal of the body at risk. Disdaining the use of the 'bot, removing the bomb-suit helmet at the first opportunity, disappearing behind a smoke screen to conduct his task alone, James seems to be seeking out a threshold or border, driven mainly by the private pleasure of excitement and fear, of living on an extreme edge.

Immediately after the death of Thompson, the EOD team is dispatched again under the leadership of James. In quick succession, the film stages several set pieces designed to emphasize the contrasts between the deceased team leader and James. In the first sequence, a pair of wires has been detected leading into a pile of trash on the street. James permits Sanborn and Eldridge, whom he is leading into the field for the first time, to outfit him with the regalia of the bomb suit before he sets off alone. As he is walking toward the location where the bomb has been sighted, under the close gaze of Sanborn and Eldridge who are charged with protecting him, he opens a smoke canister and, with a theatrical flourish, tosses it behind him on the road—a gesture that has all the drama of a diva's imperious gestures on an operatic stage. James here asserts, in effect, that this is a solo performance, and he has no need or wish for accompaniment.

The scene is staged in a way that suggests the entire city is booby-trapped and every Iraqi man is a potential assassin. Further, the jagged, discontinuous editing style creates a sense of instability and threat, as the film cuts rapidly from extreme close-up to long shot and dramatically varies the angles of view.[12] But what sets the scene apart, where its defamiliarizing accent is placed, is on the isolation of James, his solitude in a street surrounded by potential assassins. Moving away from a perspective focused on war as collective violence and collective loss, experiences that are typically crystallized in the actions and suffering of the combat team, the film concentrates instead on war as a singular, personal experience.

In a later scene, James is faced with a particularly challenging triggering device for a huge explosive hidden in a car. Puzzled by the unusual mechanism, James tries one idea after the other, as the EOD team becomes increasingly anxious. As the minutes pass, the menace increases, and Iraqi men begin noticing James and signaling to one another. Irritated by Sanborn's urgent pleas through the

James surrounded by IEDs. *The Hurt Locker,* directed by Kathryn Bigelow, 2008. Produced by Kathryn Bigelow, Mark Boal, Nicolas Chartier, and Greg Shapiro.

radio headset to abort the mission, James throws off his headset to persist in his efforts undisturbed. Elsaesser's description is exemplified here. James's drive to master a task of Daedalean complexity is matched by the pathological risk he takes in doing so, one that endangers both himself and his team—and is entirely unnecessary. As Sanborn has told him, repeatedly, they could have simply detonated the bomb remotely.

In the middle portion of the film, *The Hurt Locker* goes to some length to emphasize both James's prowess as a soldier as well as his compulsion to seek the edge, as if to nod toward convention while building toward greater and greater deviations from the cultural script. A desert combat scene, for example, provides a positive demonstration of James's more quotidian battlefield powers. In a sequence that is unusual for its echoes of the past, the EOD team comes under sniper attack and is pinned down: what ensues is a protracted working out and genre recall of one of the standard elements of the war film's plot syntax—the violent testing of the combat team and the forging of a brotherhood on the battlefield—perhaps serving to exemplify director Kathryn Bigelow's prowess in the language of genre convention.

On a training exercise in the desert, far away from the base, James, Eldridge, and Sanborn come upon a group of British mercenaries who have captured a high-level insurgent, for whom they expect a substantial bounty from the British government. The British mercenaries and the American soldiers almost immediately come under attack, pinned down by a sniper team a half mile away. Three of the mercenaries, including their leader, are quickly killed. Taking cover, James takes charge of the counterattack and locates the sniper's nest. Guided by James's telescopic spotting, Sanborn, the best rifleman on the team, shoots three enemy combatants in a patient, methodical fashion. Crucially, the young soldier Eldridge, also guided by James, contributes to the skirmish's success, using his saliva to clean the blood off the ammunition Sanborn is using, and then shooting an insurgent fighter who is about to attack from the rear.

For the first time in the film, the group is portrayed functioning as a traditional battle team, with the more experienced soldier taking the lead. Here, fighting skills, cool headedness, and James's combat leadership prevail. Moreover, Eldridge is "blooded," acquiring his first real taste of combat, and given his own lead to handle the sniper he has spotted in the distance, concealed among a herd of goats. At the end of the scene, the three soldiers share a juice pack taken from a dead mercenary's kit, an exchange that directly recalls the broken-necked bottle of wine and bloody heel of bread passed among the soldiers in the classic film *All Quiet on the Western Front* (1930) after a desperate, back-and-forth attack and retreat.

In the view of Douglas Cunningham, the desert ambush sequence constitutes the crux of the film's narrative, deploying a central convention of modernist storytelling. He describes it in terms of "the development of narrative at the level of character and emotion rather than at the level of causal action . . . the sequence . . . perform[s] the very important emotional work of foregrounding the formation of a bond among the principal characters, all of whom realize implicitly they must work effectively as a team to overcome their current threat."[13] What Cunningham does not consider, however, is the intramural violence that frames the "bonding" scene, both suggested—in the discussion between Eldridge and Sanborn at the beginning of the sequence about eliminating James, who "is going to get them killed"—and explicit, in the violence that erupts upon their return to base.

In the latter sequence, the team is shown celebrating their combat success—and their survival—in a way that has a time-honored cinematic pedigree: drinking and physically challenging one another. James and Sanborn begin testing each other's strength and ability to take a punch—what Cunningham calls a "buddy-punching contest." The roughhousing between James and Sanborn soon takes a dark, unprecedented turn, degenerating into a genuine struggle. As they wrestle on the floor, Sanborn pulls a knife from his boot and holds it to James's throat. Here, an inversion of the typical "band of brothers" communion through physical testing takes place. The sudden eruption of potentially deadly violence from within the fellowship of the team foregrounds the radical change in atmosphere that the film explores.

The scene brings past iterations of battlefield fraternity into clear visibility, only to immediately undercut the covenant on which they are based. Throughout the film, codes of representation that persist in cultural memory, artifacts of an earlier stage of genre, maintain a kind of half-life. In the gap between the conventions of the past, where embodied violence could acquire something of a redemptive, poetic shape, and the unredeemed violence of the wars of the twenty-first century, the film finds its dramatic subject and its complex mode of address.

BECKHAM

As *The Hurt Locker* progresses, the dissonance between scenarios of sacrifice and rescue that characterize earlier war films and the extraordinary forms of violence that permeate contemporary war cinema, with its body bombs and IEDs, becomes increasingly pronounced. In the film's unrelenting depiction of body trauma in war, its later scenes come close to the emotional hyperbole of Grand Guignol, combining, in a disconcerting way, the imagery of violation and waste and the heightened symbolism of an older script of the rescue narrative. As with other key moments in the film, the two scenes I address below, in which the body itself becomes a weapon of war, center on new modes of violence that modern war entails, and the film's attempt to represent these modes of violence in aesthetic form.

Ordered to investigate a report of a bomb in an abandoned warehouse, the EOD team comes upon the corpse of a boy, laid out on a table and covered in blood. His abdomen has been sliced open.

James realizes that a bomb has been planted inside the body, which upon closer inspection appears to be that of the young vendor who sold cassettes outside the base, who called himself "Beckham" and whom James had befriended. Against all procedural practice and ordinary caution, James decides to defuse and remove the bomb, sending the other team members outside as he attempts to perform a complicated operation to disable the bomb and salvage the body. Rather than simply eliminating the threat by detonating the bomb, he decides to preserve the corpse, thereby saving it from obliteration.

James's rescue of Beckham's body can easily be read as pathological risk-taking and an ideologically loaded manipulation of audience emotion, depicting grotesque body trauma in order to make a blatant political point about the villainy of the insurgency in Iraq and the American soldier's self-sacrificial willingness to risk all. From this angle, the film appears to revert to a style of stereotype characteristic of an earlier period, rendering an act of diabolical cruelty in a way that arouses an intense and highly directed emotional response. Rather than eliciting a sense of simple disgust, the image of the opened body produces a feeling of outrage, "moving the spectator," in Eisenstein's words—a case of film working directly on the somatic, emotional response of the viewer.

In the slowed tempo and closely pictured figure behavior of James, however, a secondary tone emerges. As James dismantles the bomb inside Beckham's abdomen, the act puts into a single frame the imagery of bomb defusing (its wires, leads, and secret triggers) and the imagery of surgery (organs, vessels, and flesh). James's delicate and intricate work, his skill with his hands, takes on a new meaning, as the almost tender act of working on Beckham's body brings into relief the pathos of the boy's death. Filmed in extreme close-up, the soundtrack dominated by James's breathing, the sequence culminates in his lifting the explosive from Beckham's abdomen. He then wraps the body in a white sheet and carries it from the building.

The contrast of gruesome somatic content and the sympathetic act of saving the boy's body creates an especially complex scene. On one level, the sequence brings into view the long history of representing the opened body in war, a privileged way of translating violence into meaning. In making visible the contents of the injured body, as Elaine Scarry argues, war representation lays claim to a

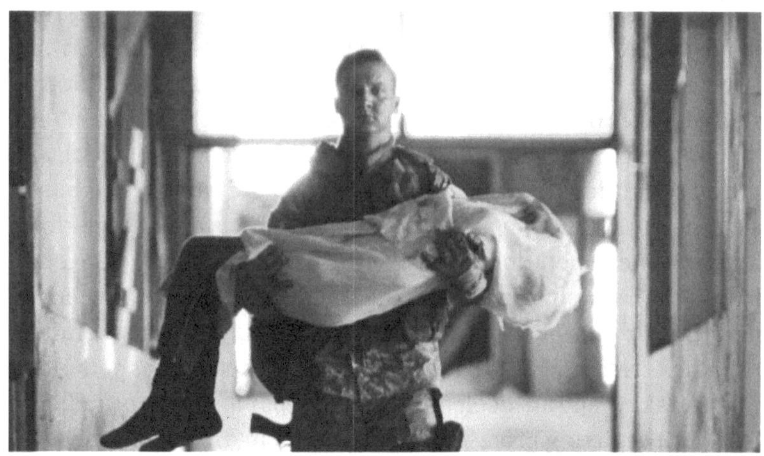

James carrying the body of an Iraqi boy. *The Hurt Locker,* directed by Kathryn Bigelow, 2008. Produced by Kathryn Bigelow, Mark Boal, Nicolas Chartier, and Greg Shapiro.

heightened symbolic authority. The power of the wounded body for representation, she writes, rests in "the mining of the ultimate substance, the ultimate source of substantiation, the extraction of the physical basis or reality from its dark hiding place in the body, out into the light of day . . . the interior content of human bodies, lungs, arteries, blood, brains, the mother lode that will eventually be reconnected to the winning issue."[14] The exposure of the secret interior, "the ultimate source of substantiation," is converted, transformed, in her view, into an icon of renewal.

In *The Hurt Locker,* however, the potent symbolism that Scarry attributes to the representation of the body, and particularly, of blood, in war is not to be found. No larger meaning can be attributed to the violence inflicted on the young boy's body, nor any sense of revelation communicated by its displayed contents. What emerges from Beckham's opened body is not some kind of ultimate "truth" of war, but rather, in a grotesque inversion, another weapon of war. Rather than an icon of regeneration and rebirth, his body speaks to a cyclical, ongoing pattern of violence and revenge.

If we shift our focus away from the display of body horror to concentrate on the poignancy of James's attempt to preserve the corpse of the dead boy, we find an equally difficult challenge to interpretation. James's act appears to be a strange variant of the rescue narrative, one of the core constellations of modern war cinema. Indeed, in the view of Elsaesser, the rescue narrative is the symbolic and emotional centerpiece of the recent American war film, providing its story armature as well as its major themes. In films such as *Saving Private Ryan* (1998), *The Deer Hunter* (1978), and *Platoon* (1986), for example, the rescue narrative shapes the major plot line and produces a psychological purgation for the main character, burdened with a bad conscience. In Elsaesser's reading, the narrative of rescue may in fact be understood as a partial corrective to the wars of conquest that have dominated American history for the past fifty years: it converts a sense of deep ambivalence into a small narrative of partial victory, concentrated in the rescue of a small group or a single soldier. As such, the medium of film itself takes on a heightened role, rescuing the past from historical guilt. The war film thus plays a reparative historical role in contemporary American life, most powerfully evidenced, Elsaesser writes, in *Saving Private Ryan.* A film riddled with retrospective guilt over the failure to rescue the Jews, in *Saving Private Ryan* the rescue of a single soldier stands as a displaced, symbolic reparation. Whether the character being rescued wishes to be saved is of little consequence: what is important is that a sense of historical guilt be transcended.[15]

In *The Hurt Locker,* however, the figure to be rescued is already dead—the victim of war has become a weapon of war, the body turned into a bomb. The overarching message inscribed in the rescue narrative in Elsaesser's reading—the conversion of historical guilt into meaningful acts that revolve around sacrifice—is somehow not available, either as communal sanction or as a rejection of the very premise that war can be meaningful. Like the opening scene of Thompson's death in the market square, the commonality of feeling, of a collective sense of the value of sacrifice or its opposite, its meaninglessness, is somehow bracketed out. The pathos of the boy's death and the emotion-laden rescue of his body is consigned, once again, to a symbolic "hurt locker" where its poignancy is registered but any larger, collective meaning is refused.

SUICIDE BOMBER

In the culminating sequence of the film, James confronts a suicide bomber. Wearing an explosive vest that guarantees death for both himself as well as his targets, the suicide bomber would appear to be the dark opposite of the armor-clad leader of the bomb disposal team, an opposition underlined by the striking differences in their combat gear. In this scene, however, the mortal antagonisms that so often define the war film are briefly suspended. The sequence, like an earlier scene in *The Hurt Locker*, obliquely recalls *All Quiet on the Western Front*. The larger, anti-war lessons of that film, however, like the other moments of genre memory that *The Hurt Locker* summons, appear mainly as a relic of the past, a distant recall of an earlier period of war cinema that persists, like an echo, in isolated scenes, detached from any semantic or social frame of meaning.

In an open city square, with dozens of spectators ringing the blast zone, a middle-aged man dressed in a black suit stands at the center. Calling out in Arabic, he begs to be released from the explosive vest into which he has been locked. The Iraqi translator assigned to the mission tells James, repeatedly and with conviction, "He is a family man, he is a good man," as he relays the words of the bomber, who says that he has four children. The translator explains that the man was forced by the insurgency to wear the vest and that he does not want to die. James and Sanborn approach the man, pistols drawn, and discover that the vest is made of metal ribs with numerous padlocks holding it together. It is also wired to a timer, which shows only minutes until the bomb will detonate.

James tries to calm the man and tells him he will help. But the bomb is too complicated to defuse in the minutes remaining, and the bolt cutters he uses are not able to cut through the case-hardened steel of the padlocks. James persists in trying to rescue the man. Sanborn pleads with James to retreat, saying "He's a dead man, James, leave him!" James orders Sanborn to safety and tries again. He apologizes to the bomber, "I can't. I'm sorry. There are too many locks! I'm sorry! I'm sorry!" At the last moment James runs to the perimeter, as the man, on his knees praying, arms outstretched, is blown to shreds.

The sequence is a distant echo of one of the most famous scenes in war cinema, the battlefield encounter in the deep shell crater in *All Quiet on the Western Front*. In the classic film, the young German protagonist, Paul Bäumer (Lew Ayres), apologizes at length to the French soldier he has stabbed in combat, who is slowly dying in the hole—a scene that has been lauded for its psychological depth and

James trying to free an unwilling suicide bomber from his explosive vest. *The Hurt Locker*, directed by Kathryn Bigelow, 2008. Produced by Kathryn Bigelow, Mark Boal, Nicolas Chartier, and Greg Shapiro.

the power of its anti-war message. After the soldier dies, Paul finds the soldier's ID card and pictures of his family in his wallet and promises to write to them after the war. The sequence, which unfolds at a deliberate pace, is dominated by Paul's increasing recognition of their similarities and by the fact that they have been forced into the role of enemies.

In *The Hurt Locker*, the camera work and the figure behavior of both the suicide bomber and James carry a similar but variant message. Throughout the harrowing sequence, the film emphasizes the humanity of the bomber with a number of dramatic close-ups, and underlines James's increasing desperation as the camera follows his attempts to free the bomber from the vest. A close-up of James's flexing hand as he tries to think of a solution alternates with quick shots of the Iraqi's face. At one point, both characters grasp each other's arms, seemingly locked in an embrace. Staged at a tachycardic pace, the scene is suffused with cinematic adrenalin; fast zooms, rapid cuts, Sanborn's shouting as he tries to force James to abandon the Iraqi—the tempo is ratcheted up as the seconds tick down. Condensing an extreme range of emotional signals, the sequence's images and sounds elicit a sense of heightened sympathy for the doomed man while simultaneously conveying an almost violent somatic tension as the action builds.

As I have suggested above, the scene obliquely recalls *All Quiet on the Western Front,* in which enmity yields to a feeling of mutual existential risk, a sense of both characters sharing a common fate. The emotional vector of the sequence from the older film is straightforward—a full-throated rejection of war's violence. In *The Hurt Locker,* by contrast, the emotion generated by the scene is complex. The close-up shooting style, the pleading figure behavior of the Iraqi man, the lighting of his face and hands—the pathos of his imminent death gives his last moments of connection with James a particular poignancy. But it also carries a secondary accent. The violence of the death scene registers as both tragic and spectacular, overpoweringly visceral. The combination of close-up, tactile imagery and the extravagant tableau of the Iraqi's immolation move the larger consideration of social meaning to the background. And directly after the scene concludes, James confesses that he has no idea why he does what he does: the empathy he shows to the Iraqi victim seems like a free-floating, momentary emotion, untethered to any larger sense of the waste and tragedy of war.

For all its contemporaneity, *The Hurt Locker* is in many ways a deeply historical text, engaging with the history of war representation in film while at the same time refusing the symbolic solutions that create the "feeling of commonality" described by Kappelhoff. In this chapter, I have argued that the film both evokes and undercuts the iconic themes of the war film, a genre whose conventions, in the view of Robert Eberwein, were established in the first years of the cinema.[16] Although several of the defining themes and motifs of the genre—the rescue scenario, the bond of brotherhood forged in battle, the mourning for a fallen comrade—are foregrounded in *The Hurt Locker,* they are bent into different shapes. Their role as consoling scripts that reinforce the notion of an imagined community, of a "deep, horizontal kinship" of nation, is negated, even reversed, turned into expressions of solitude and loss.[17] Perhaps even more striking, the contrary themes of the anti-war film—war as rampant waste, depravity, and desolation—are likewise unavailable as interpretive possibilities. Instead, the film repeatedly sets the stage for the unfolding of one or another of these narrative paradigms, as

Bigelow provides familiar genre reference points and then reworks the script from a new and unfamiliar perspective.

The overall project of the film is also quite different from what Elsaesser and others describe as the cinematic rescue of the past, exemplified by films such as *Saving Private Ryan*—a redemptive filmic writing of history meant to assuage contemporary guilt. In a national context of continuous, relentless, and often illegitimate warfare in parts of the world that pose little existential or economic threat to the United States, the reclaiming of a small-scale, fictional achievement—such as the rescue of Ryan or the survival of the young soldier in the World War II film *Fury* (2014)—no longer serves to momentarily restore to visibility an older triumphal narrative of nation. Contemporary films set in current conflict zones, such as *The Hurt Locker,* seem far removed from these kinds of narrative agendas.

In contrast, *The Hurt Locker,* I argue, evokes the older codes and conventions of the war film as a memory, a set of references that are called up and then swept away by the new forms of violent encounter, the grammars of violence that contemporary war entails. The film evokes images and scenarios that at one time triggered a deep sense of recognition—scenes of heroic self-sacrifice, the burial and mourning of a fallen comrade, a rescue operation that arrives too late—but it refuses to track these emotions into a recognizable cultural script. The pathos the film arouses, as powerful as the most exemplary war films of the past, is detached, disconnected from any larger rhetorical or symbolic meaning. As Fredric Jameson once wrote, "History is what hurts."[18] Here, the hurt and anguish of war is evoked and at the same time suppressed, aroused but refused any symbolic resolution. What *The Hurt Locker* conveys is rather an extraordinary sense of both the external and internal registers of violence in war—violence that has come to define the young century so far, as well as the subjectivities shaped within it.

CHAPTER 2

WAITING FOR TERROR

Zero Dark Thirty

THE VIOLENCE THAT *ZERO DARK THIRTY* (2012) explores from its initial moments to its deflating conclusion is at once intimate, personal, and inseparable from the large-scale violence that dominates the short history of the young century. In the course of the film, violence is rendered in immediate close-up, both acoustic and visual, and gradually dilated to read as a defining historical motif, an "organizing cultural and aesthetic fact," as the literary historian Sarah Cole writes in another context.[1] Rendering the concrete terror of 9/11 in an acoustic montage, followed by a brutal depiction of interrogation and torture, *Zero Dark Thirty* appears to rehearse a pattern film scholar Jonna Eagle has discerned in twentieth-century American culture and history, where the experience of victimization and the feeling of vulnerability mobilizes extreme forms of spectacular, retributive violence. As depicted in the film, the attacks of 9/11 triggered an exorbitant enactment of punitive agency, seeming to illustrate the recto–verso of vulnerability and imagined omnipotence described in Eagle's work.[2] Unlike earlier representations, however, the imaginative potency of spectacular force, its symbolic power, has faded away. In the portrait of terror and counterterror offered in *Zero Dark Thirty*, retributive violence has been drained of its imaginative and symbolic value.

The film details the CIA's search for Osama bin Laden in the years after 9/11, depicting the decade-long effort to track him down, efforts that included the interrogation and torture of hundreds of suspected members of al-Qaeda. A young CIA agent, Maya (Jessica

Chastain), provides the film's focalizing perspective and serves as the principal narrative agent. Introduced during her first experience of what was euphemistically called "enhanced interrogation," Maya enters the film as a wide-eyed witness who quickly becomes an effective agent—intelligent, creative, and implacable. Eventually, Maya is placed in charge of the CIA search for bin Laden, which has narrowed to the effort to identify and track his courier, Shaykh Abu Ahmed al Kuwaiti, a figure who proves extremely elusive. After years of searching, the CIA team—led by Maya—finally succeeds in tracking Abu Ahmed to what may be bin Laden's compound in Pakistan. An elaborate procedure to confirm the presence of bin Laden in the compound is then set in motion. In the closing act of the film, a team of Navy SEALs conduct a nocturnal raid on the complex—a clockwork exercise in choreographed violence, culminating in the killing of Osama bin Laden. When the SEAL team returns, Maya is called on to identify the body. In the final shot of the film, she is pictured alone, in close-up, aboard an Air Force troop carrier whose pilot has been instructed to take her anywhere she wants to go.

With Maya driving the pursuit of bin Laden, a picture of a hidden world emerges, one defined by secret networks and threats that may or may not be real, where a sense of ontological uncertainty and fear prevails—underlined by scenes of visceral injury, death, and violent confrontation. The shock and horror of the surprise attack of 9/11 frames the film, which opens with a montage of the voices of victims and the voice of a police dispatcher rendered over a black screen, plunging the viewer into a moment that is both known and unknown, radically defamiliarizing an event that had become almost a visual cliché. Crafting its depiction of 9/11 in a way that penetrates the veil of familiarity that has formed around the events, the film uses the actual soundtrack of victims' recorded voices as a sonic shorthand for a historical experience that has eluded effective representation. The voices of 9/11, as presented in the film, are a document of the victims' trauma, placing physical experience at the center of an event that had grown encrusted by repetition. The opening scene positions the audience as acoustic witness in a way that both short-circuits the voyeurism often elicited by the imagery of disaster and collapses the distancing that visual representation often allows.

The black screen that opens the film, however, also suggests another reading, reminding us, with its empty field of vision, that the bodies of the victims as well as the bodies of the perpetrators simply disappeared in the collapse of the towers. The mass murder of 9/11, the most filmed and viewed event in history, was, strangely, a disembodied event. For some writers, the absence of bodies, of both the perpetrators and the victims, had an almost uncanny effect. As Cole writes, "The visual spectacles of 9/11 have been seen by billions, but with the exception of a few stunning photographs featuring falling bodies . . . no one has ever seen the bodies of the dead. The violence of the attacks was instantly recognized as historic and transformative, and the absence of flesh made its own imaginative claims."[3] The invisibility of the perpetrators, moreover, heightened the sense of disorientation. Describing the attacks of 9/11 as a "crisis of violence and the visible," Anne McClintock writes that the suicide attackers, in obliterating themselves, removed their bodies "from the realm of visible retribution," and therefore deprived the Bush administration of the means to recover its potency. "The state was faced with an immediate dilemma: how to embody the invisible enemy and be visibly seen to punish it?"[4]

In *Zero Dark Thirty*, what McClintock calls the "crisis of violence and the visible" following the attacks of 9/11 frames the first third of the film. In its opening scenes, the film directly connects the spectacle of the punished body—the detailed rendering of torture by the CIA—with the near invisibility of terror networks, casting bin Laden and his courier Abu Ahmed as will-o'-the-wisp characters whose elusiveness generates extreme forms of compensatory violence. In an unprecedented move in war cinema, however, the film casts the figure of Maya, a young woman seemingly new to the job, as the principal agent of state violence, introducing her, in medias res, in the middle of a sordid interrogation.

MAYA

The film's challenge to the dominant paradigms of war cinema begins in the interrogation scene that opens the first full act. Here, Maya, whose youth and inexperience are initially foregrounded, quickly progresses from reluctant witnessing to coercive agency. Covering her eyes, clutching her jacket, forcing herself to watch—then surprisingly demanding that they "go back in"—Maya is foregrounded in the scene's shot patterning. The act of witnessing, ordinarily conceived in more anodyne terms, is here shown to be inseparable from agency, as Maya's witnessing of torture becomes a tool of torture—a point that is scenically presented in a series of close-ups and eye-line matches among Maya, the interrogator Dan (Jason Clarke), and the torture victim Ammar (Reda Kateb).

To a certain extent, Maya serves as a surrogate for the spectator, the focalizing prism through whom we experience the brutality of torture, a character who first averts her eyes, followed by an incremental hardening of attitude and sense. The formal patterning of the first torture scene locks the character into an unwanted, intimate relation with the prisoner, metonymically connecting her to the injured body, not by touch, but by the gaze. It is her gaze that is evoked as he is paraded naked from the waist down and then walked around the room like a dog; it is her gaze that holds the power to humiliate; and it is her gaze that Dan consults before he continues the torture. The surprising thing here is the intimacy that flows from the scene: she is connected to the victim in a way that has the paradoxical effect of humanizing him; rather than creating a barrier, the injury and mortification of the body—and her viewing of it—creates a join between the characters, a point that comes through strongly when she is alone with him in the cell. Similar in age, their relationship not yet patterned by the grammars of violence that organize the interrogation procedure, the victim asks Maya to help him, to spare him from her partner, who is a "madman." For a moment, what has sometimes been described as the strange intimacy between oppressor and victim surfaces, with the two characters facing each other in what Paul Virilio calls the half-light of war: "War is a symptom of delirium operating in the half-light of trance, drugs, blood and unison. This half-light establishes a corporeal identity in the clinch of allies and enemies, victims and executioners."[5] Here too, the observer becomes the observed, as the character of Maya is scrutinized, closely appraised by the spectator, by the lead interrogator, and by the victim himself.

Maya represents a new type of protagonist in the long history of the war film—in ways that extend beyond her gender. In previous films featuring female soldiers—*Courage under Fire* (1996) and *GI Jane*

(1997) come immediately to mind—the lead characters are "masculinized," in the words of Yvonne Tasker, assuming the language, gestures, and controlled aggressiveness conventionally associated with male war film characters. Maya, by contrast, seems utterly indifferent to the visible signs of gendered behavior. Gifted, driven, almost asocial, and utterly focused on the pursuit of bin Laden, she has none of the characteristics of the charismatic hero, nor is she portrayed as a figure of emotional depth or range. Unlike the character of Sergeant William James, whom I described in the previous chapter as exhibiting a pronounced form of what Thomas Elsaesser has called productive pathology, Maya is addicted neither to combat danger nor to the thrill of the chase. Yet she pursues bin Laden with a single-mindedness that seems preternatural. And her willingness to do the dirty work eclipses that of her male colleagues. As agent and mirror of violence, however, Maya disturbs the usual operative models in film. Pre-Raphaelite in her beauty, she conveys contradictory messages associated with the violence of contemporary war. The character's youth and sculpted beauty troubles the paradigm of purposive violence, underlining the discordance between her physical appearance and her role, or better, her vocation.[6] As her CIA station chief remarks when asked if she is too young for this kind of assignment, "She's a killer. That's what Washington says."[7]

Although Maya as protagonist represents a striking departure from war cinema convention, director Kathryn Bigelow goes well beyond the creation of a singular and unique figure, building in a surprising density of female presence in the world the film depicts. In the acoustic montage that opens the film, for example, the voices of the victims of 9/11 resolve into a dialogue exchange between one terrified woman trapped in the towers and a female dispatcher at the police station, whom she has called for help. More significantly, when Maya is first assigned to her CIA post, she immediately meets a senior female agent, Jessica Karley (Jennifer Ehle), with whom she forms a friendship. As Jessica pursues a dangerous meeting at the CIA outpost at Camp Chapman in Afghanistan with a possible informant, Maya and she are in constant communication via text. Another young female agent, moreover, assists Jessica at the meeting. And after the search for the true name of bin Laden's courier seems to have gone cold, it is a female agent—who says she has admired

Maya's work for years—who discovers a photograph and pieces together the actual name of the courier, information that the young agent brings to Maya rather than to a senior male agent. Finally, the several women in bin Laden's compound are depicted as silent and anonymous but potentially lethal: one reaches for her husband's rifle during the raid and is promptly killed by the American soldiers. The shift in gender roles that is such a striking aspect of many of the war films I consider here extends beyond the protagonist roles to suggest a wider culture of war that now includes, and in some cases foregrounds, female operatives.

DISENCHANTED VIOLENCE

As the film unfolds, the interrogation videos that Maya watches over and over, spread out on her computer screens in a frightening, Goya-like montage of gasping, shackled men, pushes the connection between witnessing and violent infliction to the center of the film's pictorial vocabulary. Studying the interrogations, rewinding and replaying scenes of prisoners shackled to the ceiling, handcuffed to tables, thrown to the floor, or sitting without visible restraint, the character hears—or imagines she hears—the name "Abu Ahmed," the courier's nom de guerre, repeated again and again, a name that sometimes emerges from the questioning and is sometimes supplied by the interrogator. Maya's face, reflected in the computer monitor or viewed in profile as the voices and sounds of the interrogation proceed, is the scene's presiding focus, her expression of intense concentration seeming to belie the horror of the history of violence summarized in these clips. As Maya drills deep into the cassettes, mouthing the words "Abu Ahmed" when the victims of torture are unable to speak clearly, the courier's pseudonym comes to seem like an incantation, drawing her in. At one point she is shown walking into sunlight from the dark interior of the office, moving slowly and distractedly into bright light, only to return immediately to the violent interrogations unfolding on her computer screen. Finally, she brings up the image of a noticeably young man, framed in close-up, who tells the interrogator that there are many couriers and that no one knows who is directly in contact with bin Laden. His youth, his look of boyish openness, his obvious fear, all seem to call out for empathy. Maya's response is ambiguous, peering at his frozen image, her face half blackened by shadow.

In the interrogation scenes depicted in the film, the need to embody the invisible enemy, "and be visibly seen to punish it," in McClintock's words, is presented in graphic, squalid detail, bringing into close proximity the act of witnessing and the experience of bodily violation. Surrounded by videos, with materials stacked high on every surface, Maya flips between screens and cassettes with ease. The institutional status of torture during this period is underlined in an offhand way here, communicated by the piles of cassettes and the multiple screens Maya watches, "normalized," to use Slavoj Žižek's term—a point that is highlighted in the direct cut from a torture scene to a toaster popping out a piece of bread in the scene that follows.[8]

The history of the war film is marked by innovations in the vocabulary of violence, moments when new cinematic forms have emerged in response to the radically changing sensory experience of war. The extraordinary tracking shots and sound design of *All Quiet on the Western Front* (1930), for example, took shape as a formal strategy cued to the brutality of World War I. The film offered an intensive somatic reenactment that was also a formal solution to the problem of representing the unprecedented violence of mechanized war. The D-Day landing sequence in *Saving Private Ryan* (1998), for another example, bound the excessive, gruesome violence of the landing on Omaha Beach to an intricate filmic design that merged traumatized perception and documentary realism. And in *Apocalypse Now* (1979), the tight connection between violence and aesthetic form gave rise to the most unsettling forms and images of beauty, such as the surround sound helicopter attack and flaming jungles of Colonel Kilgore's raid on a quiet Vietnam village in the first third of the film, as well as scenes of macabre fascination, as in the grotesque body landscapes of Colonel Kurtz's compound—sequences that have come to serve as memory triggers for the destructiveness and pathology of the Vietnam War. In short, the violence of war, its intensity and scale, seems to excite potent aesthetic responses.

Zero Dark Thirty, I argue, explores a new vocabulary of violence in contemporary war, initially shaping its treatment around the character of Maya, then focusing on the Navy SEALs, and setting out an imaginative structure that can best be described as a new articulation of "enchanted" and "disenchanted" violence—a dichotomy I am borrowing from Sarah Cole. Focusing on an earlier period—the response of Modernist poets and novelists to the devastating violence of World War I—Cole argues that violence, especially violence inflicted on the body, is conceived in Modernist literature as either enchanted or disenchanted, as the "germinating core of rich symbolic structures," or the "emblem of grotesque loss"; as a symbol of historical transformation and renewal, or as a sign of utter degeneration and waste: "To enchant, in this sense, is to imbue the violent experience with symbolic and cultural potency; to disenchant is to refuse that structure, to insist on the bare, forked existence of the violated being, bereft of symbol."[9]

With the violated body coming into sharp figurative and dramatic focus in the first third of the film, *Zero Dark Thirty* appears to place visceral violence at the center of representation, underlining physical experience—the extreme, haptic shock of torture and the sudden eruption of terror—as the emblematic expressions of contemporary war. The intimacy of torture, rendered in scenes of violent infliction, provides a particularly vivid expression of what Cole calls disenchanted violence; the hard lighting, unadorned camera work, and static, low-resolution optics of the interrogation videos speak directly to themes of violence as degeneracy and waste. Focusing on the flesh, refusing to idealize or glamourize the war on terror or burnish it with patriotic appeal, the film renders the events of 9/11 and its aftermath in a form that is brutal and direct—as Cole writes, "bereft of symbol." The aestheticizing of violence through form, the almost ceremonial stylization that accompanies many scenes of embodied violence in film, is simply not found in these sequences.

The film pivots into more familiar genre convention, however, with the killing of Maya's CIA colleague Jessica, a woman who had befriended Maya and whose warmth and humanity set her apart. With this devastating scene, rendered in a style of exacting suspense, "violence can find its conventions," as Cole writes. Set in a remote desert base in Afghanistan, the scene plays a set of emotional keys distinct from what has gone before, emphasizing Jessica's optimism, her excitement at meeting a purported "mole" who has offered to sell his access and his information, and reinforcing the emotion by crosscutting to Maya at the CIA base in Pakistan.

As the possible contact is driven to the camp, the sequence builds anticipation, rendering the drawn-out transit of his vehicle through the desert in extreme long shot as it approaches the outer perimeter of the base. Cutting between Jessica, the interior of the vehicle as it moves into the camp, and Maya at her computer in Pakistan, the film links Maya and her CIA colleague sharing the excitement and anticipation of their "first big break since 9/11." At Jessica's insistence, and in violation of the rules, the contact is allowed to pass the checkpoint and is admitted into the interior of the camp without being searched. As the man exits the car, the editing gains pace and intensity, and the shot sizes shift to a series of jagged close-ups. As his body bomb detonates, the film cuts to a single high-level shot of the explosion. It then cuts back to Maya, sitting at her computer, her face suffused with anxiety as Jessica has stopped sending messages.

Maya serves as focalizer of this sequence, her emotions of excitement, anxiety, and dread coloring and accenting the action. A hinge point in the narrative, the scene foregrounds the emotions of a character whose inner life has been opaque. It also marks the beginning of the film's second segment, as the brutal and radically disenchanting interrogations that dominate the first third give way to the genre language of the procedural, a cinematic accommodation that shifts away from Maya's violent administrations of torture to a form that accesses the familiar conventions of popular drama.

THE PROCEDURAL

In the film's middle portion, *Zero Dark Thirty* turns the question of "how to produce the enemy as bodies?" into a procedural, with wall-sized displays of headshots of possible terrorist leaders, some with large X's drawn on their faces, graphic illustrations of crisscrossed lines of connection, and an elaborate display of surveillance imagery and cell phone data filling the foreground of the text. Torture as a technique recedes from view in the film's second act, as it did from the CIA's fieldwork after President Barack Obama, on his first day in office, denounced the practice and ended the policy. With its move into the cyber mapping of terror, the film's depiction of the manhunt changes from physical surveillance and interrogation to an electronic dragnet, aided by street-level operatives—a search that involves networks of satellite surveillance, cell phone tracking, human observers in the cities of Pakistan, and multiple agencies, marshaled into a vast and hierarchical intelligence apparatus. As Eileen Rositzka describes it, "The film itself seems to establish virtual spaces that develop a life of their own. . . . The sequence thus becomes a metaphor for a communication network that is too complex to grasp by means of human perception, but one that is governed by an unmistakable—and unforgiving—technological construct."[10]

Caught up in the friction and overlap of contradictory interpretations, competing agencies, and differing agendas that are their own raison d'être, the search for bin Laden becomes subsumed into a hyper-rationalized process that, although intriguing, seems far from the urgent focus the film had established in its first third. But here a striking shift in Maya's narrative status and characterization takes hold. In the earlier portion of the film, her dedication to the dark arts of warfare, her full participation in the most objectionable forms of coercive interrogation, had begun to coalesce into a highly critical portrait, as if the contaminating force of violence had created an internally deformed being, a creature who, despite her beauty and intelligence, is somehow only half human. In the middle portion of the film, however, Maya becomes the full-fledged heroine of the drama, commanding our rooting interest—a character that stands up to bureaucracy, pushes the pursuit forward with aggressiveness and purpose, and maintains her exacting commitment to the mission in the face of bureaucratic timidity and skepticism. In a briefing session with CIA director Leon Panetta (James Gandolfini), Maya, the only woman in the room, asserts her absolute certainty that bin Laden is resident in the compound; using vulgar language, she claims firsthand authorship of the successful identification of the courier, Abu Ahmed, and full credit for tracking him to the hideout. She dismisses the careerist caution of the males in the room, who seem most interested in hedging their bets. To the extent that she can, she shreds protocol and convention and persists in driving the bin Laden mission forward.

Maya, marking the days of the long wait for the raid on bin Laden's compound to begin. *Zero Dark Thirty*, directed by Kathryn Bigelow, 2012. Produced by Kathryn Bigelow, Mark Boal, and Megan Ellison.

Maya's change in narrative status underlines the significance of the procedural, its function as an "ideologeme," in Fredric Jameson's sense, in the film's textual arrangement.[11] The procedural has become one of the signature genres of contemporary television and film, and in its middle sequences *Zero Dark Thirty* seems to fit, at least in part, the generic outlines of this form of popular drama, detailing the forensic analysis, high-level strategizing, and careful modeling of various scenarios that defined the pursuit of bin Laden in this phase of the operation. As Steven Shaviro has described it, the procedural emphasizes process and analysis in its narrative design, but more importantly, it elevates process to an overarching value, independent of any particular end or goal. For Shaviro, proceduralism is the characteristic mode of social and political organization in contemporary life, the late, entropic expression of liberal capitalism, where the achievement of positive ends, such as social justice, are secondary to the administration of procedural regularity and order: "*Zero Dark Thirty* is the ne plus ultra of proceduralism, its ultimate expansion and reductio ad absurdum. . . . The premise and initial impetus of this process is of course the mythological demonization of Bin Laden, as the ultimate culprit responsible for Nine Eleven. But in the relentless proceduralism that the film presents to us, this goal or rationale is abraded away."[12] His short, powerful analysis describes the dissolution of narrative energy and dynamism in the film, its deliberate draining of dramatic action into data and process: "The film makes a sort of feint by implying that its real subject is the passion of its protagonist Maya. . . . But her obsession is itself entirely contained within, and articulated by, the proceduralism which is her job as a CIA analyst, and which seems to be the only world she knows."[13]

The second act of *Zero Dark Thirty,* with its fact-checking, cross-referencing of data, satellite surveillance, and digital graphs of voice recordings, manifests many of the characteristics described by Shaviro. The mechanisms of intelligence gathering are rendered in exacting detail, with internal debates marking each incremental step in the process. Diffuse rather than concentrated, the drama and tension generated in the extended middle portion of the film is spread out through multiple networks of government agencies, electronic tracking systems, remote and ground-level surveillance. Cross cutting between fraught, closed-room meetings at CIA headquarters and tense street scenes in Peshawar and Rawalpindi, the film conveys a full sense of the complexity and weight of the dragnet operation constructed to find bin Laden.

Rather than subsiding into what Shaviro describes as an empty, enervating emphasis on process for its own sake, however, the middle sequences of the film might rather be seen as indexing a historical change—the rapid escalation and increasing penetration of intelligence operations, following a long period in which intelligence networks had been actively downgraded. As Mark Bowden writes, "An intelligence network like America's is not one but multiple bureaucracies, each with its own specialty—listening, observing, photographing, sensing, probing, analyzing. . . . The new tool was everything: reconstituted human spy networks, supercomputers, state-of-the-art software, global surveillance, and elite commando units."[14]

The detailed and intricate portrayal of the intelligence apparatus depicted in these scenes also reflects the unprecedented access to information obtained by the filmmakers. Highly regarded for *The Hurt Locker* within the Defense establishment, director Kathryn Bigelow and screenwriter Mark Boal were allowed to interview many high-level CIA officers and given physical access to areas of CIA headquarters, and to CIA ceremonies, that were off-limits to outsiders. The

Maya watching on her computer the raid on bin Laden's compound. *Zero Dark Thirty*, directed by Kathryn Bigelow, 2012. Produced by Kathryn Bigelow, Mark Boal, and Megan Ellison.

cooperation of the CIA in the making of the film allowed Bigelow and Boal to say that their portrayal of events was based on interviews with people who had firsthand knowledge of the pursuit and killing of bin Laden. As one essay describes it, "The agency . . . arranged for the filmmakers to have access to the 'vault'—the room where much of the Navy SEALs' tactical planning occurred. . . . More importantly, the CIA's Office of Public Affairs set up multiple meetings for Boal and Bigelow with people who could offer expert, inside information on the long search for bin Laden."[15]

The violence at the film's core is somewhat concealed in the middle portion by the grinding, deliberate pace of bureaucratic machinery, but it emerges undisguised in the language of the agency, in particular, in the speech of Maya. Her almost religious zeal—"I believe I was spared so I can finish the job," she says at one point—is an iteration of violence that is barely contained by the procedural focus. At several points the CIA operatives end their discussions with matter-of-fact statements like "And if he doesn't, we kill him"; "I want targets. Bring me people to kill"; or Maya's chilling line "I'm going to smoke everyone involved in this op, and then I'm going to kill bin Laden." The power of violence in this scenario, its penetrating and contaminating imaginative potency, permeates the middle of the film, reframing the narrative in a way that sets the intelligence apparatus of technologized, networked violence against the master narrative of jihad promoted by bin Laden and al-Qaeda.

ENCHANTED VIOLENCE

The first third of the film, concentrating on the victims of terror and the victims of torture, depicts violence as radically disenchanted, providing a close-up view, acoustic and visual, of the experience of bodily violation. Rendered in a harsh, flat style, the grim interrogation scenes of *Zero Dark Thirty* can be seen, as Cole has it, to "strip away from the violated body all forms of symbolic valorization," and to stand against any ideal of violence as "purifying or cathartic."[16] In its climactic scenes, however, a new vocabulary of enchanted violence comes to the fore. The nighttime raid on bin Laden's compound, conducted by a crack team of Navy SEALs, is staged as a choreographed incursion, more reminiscent of the graceful attack protocols of aerial combat than the desperate struggle against the elements and the enemy that characterize ground operations in most war films. Moving in concert with central command, operating from a finely calibrated plan of attack, supported by a vast technological apparatus, the SEALs here embody a heightened, almost aesthetic proficiency. Violence, in the final third of *Zero Dark Thirty,* is enchanted into art.[17]

In the film, however, the raid on bin Laden's compound has nothing of the organic, generative character that Cole describes as characteristic of enchanted violence in the earlier years of the twentieth century, where the poets of World War I often wove together death, nature, and the imagery of germinal renewal. Nevertheless, the raid does—briefly—suggest something like a sense of transformation, of violence wresting visible order and meaning from the darkness of 9/11. In the climactic scenes of the film, violence is rendered as a virtuoso performance in which, for a moment, the specter of terror is expunged.

In contrast to the harsh realism of the torture scenes, the nocturnal raid explores a new, visually surprising aesthetic, with the green light of the night vision goggles of the SEAL team providing images that are striking and spectacular. The special ops raid on bin Laden's

Night vision optics, the raid on bin Laden's compound. *Zero Dark Thirty*, directed by Kathryn Bigelow, 2012. Produced by Kathryn Bigelow, Mark Boal, and Megan Ellison.

compound can be seen as a particularly charged expression of enchanted violence, freighted with metaphoric and symbolic meaning, in which the vocabulary of technology, teamwork, and the raison d'être of the "mission" is coded as transformative and redemptive. As agents of enchanted violence in the twenty-first century, the Navy SEAL unit that conducts the raid is exemplary: decked out in technology, auditing and communicating information in a continuous stream, otherworldly in their skill and discipline, the SEALs team casts aside the ordinary world of disenchanted violence—the deforming violence of war. Instead, we see their doubled night vision goggles and armored body suits, replete with an array of weapons and tools that materialize when needed—like a Batsuit with lethal implements. We see their instantaneous and correct decisions, and their gentleness with the children in the compound. We see their quick dispatch of potential threats, and we linger not over the bodies they have left behind but rather over the computer hard drives they collect. The awful violence of war, and the physical reality of the mission with its blood and bodies, is mitigated and transformed into art in this sequence. Although the grisly effects of war are asserted in the details, like the smear of blood left behind on the floor when bin Laden's body is dragged away, and the hard-to-watch shooting of a woman who throws herself over the body of her dead husband while reaching for his rifle, the overarching impact of this scene is one of sustained, intense physical excitement.

EXORCISM

As the film draws to its conclusion, however, a very different set of themes comes to the fore, a kind of modulation to a minor key. Andrew Hill writes that over the ten years of the search, the figure of bin Laden had assumed the status of what he calls an "anamorphic ghost," a demonic figure haunting the imagination of the West, an elusive spectral being whose location in physical space, in the Real, could not be verified. The uncanny, haunting effect of the grainy video and voice recordings he periodically released, along with the failure of U.S. intelligence agencies to generate any confirmed sightings of bin Laden, created a sense of demonic presence, a figure able to appear and disappear at will, haunting the borderlands, whose malign influence made him seem omnipresent. The decision by the Obama administration not to release any photographs of bin Laden's corpse, along with his quick burial at sea, can be seen as a response, Hill writes, to the fiendish power the figure had attained in the Western Imaginary. The erasure of his body served as a kind of exorcism—a killing in the Symbolic as well as a killing in the Real. Referencing Jacques Derrida, Hill writes, "The Obama administration sought to utilize Operation Neptune Spear to perform another function as well—namely, a type of exorcism . . . 'seeking to deprive the ghost, of any interstice, lodging, or space favourable to haunting.'" And summarizing Jacques Lacan and Žižek, Hill explains the actions of the Obama administration as an effort to annul the symbolic status of bin Laden, as "striving to bring about his second, Symbolic death."[18]

The closing scenes of *Zero Dark Thirty* suggest some of the themes described above. As the SEAL team delivers the body and the computer files taken from the compound back to the desert staging camp, the excitement of having accomplished the mission is initially visible among the soldiers. Congratulating one another, working at speed to sort the documents and hard drives, the adrenalin still palpable in their voices and gestures, the SEALs share a collective moment of exhilaration. The body in its bag is almost forgotten, pushed

Maya after identifying the body of bin Laden. *Zero Dark Thirty,* directed by Kathryn Bigelow, 2012. Produced by Kathryn Bigelow, Mark Boal, and Megan Ellison.

to the side as an object of interest. The camera then cuts to Maya, alone, outside on the runway. As she makes her way into the crowded tent, the camera picks her out, walking slowly through the team of men toward the body bag. The soldiers part for her and become quiet as she moves among them, as if the darkness momentarily expiated by the successful mission had returned. As she approaches the corpse, the camera switches to a low-angle view. In the medium eye-level shot that follows, she unzips the bag. She confirms the identity of the corpse to the commanding officer, who transmits the information via telephone to an unheard recipient (presumably President Obama). She looks back at the body, zips up the bag, and walks slowly out the back of the tent.

The film conceals bin Laden's face from the camera, staging the identification of bin Laden in a muted visual style, purging it of drama or affect—a second, Symbolic death. But rather than blood satisfaction or triumphalism, the scene communicates a tone of uneasy ambivalence—just at a point when we had expected a crescendo of emotion. In some ways we are suspended here, without resolution, without the climax that the film had prepared from the beginning. Although the first third of the film seemed to be devoted to producing the enemy as bodies, and to visibly punishing those enemies, the unusual and surprising final scenes of the work conceal from our view the face of the primal enemy. And in the closing shot of the film, which functions like a coda, the theme of suspension, of lack of closure, is made explicit. From inside a large transport plane, a cargo door opens to view Maya on the runway, framed against a breaking dawn. She enters the plane and the cargo door closes. The young pilot tells her she is the only one on the plane and asks where she would like to go. A close-up of Maya follows, a portraiture shot almost a minute in length, as the question hangs in the air, and her tears begin to flow.[19] Ambiguous and strangely unsettling, the shot of Maya seems to signify neither an ending nor a beginning, but rather an uneasy waiting, a pause point in an unfolding narrative without resolution.

Zero Dark Thirty portrays the violence of counterterrorism partly as a response to an epistemological crisis, with speculation, imaginative projection, and a heightened sense of uncertainty crosshatching every narrative event. The construction of possible story worlds, usually the province of a fictional narrator in a novel, emerges here as the defining mode of practice in the intelligence community, whose techniques of analysis have been reshaped by what Secretary of Defense Donald Rumsfeld called the "unknown unknowns" of terror. Beginning with the first interrogation scene and continuing through the planning for the assault on the compound, the terror scenarios that the film's characters pursue and anticipate are marked by speculation. As Richard Jackson writes, "Security officials have come to focus on the 'unknown' element of terrorism. . . . This represents the adoption of ontological uncertainty as a fundamental condition of terrorism knowledge, in effect, severing links to previous empirical evidence, analytical frameworks, and knowledge, and remaking terrorism as an unlimited and infinite risk."[20]

To a certain extent, the film's singular focus on the pursuit and killing of bin Laden, its foregrounding of this one individual strand of the growing spider web of terror, may be seen as symbolic, an attempt to master, in narrative form, the ontological uncertainty that pervades the contemporary war on terror. Understood as a symbolic resolution, the killing of bin Laden can be read as throwing a thin line across the void of meaning surrounding terrorism, a void that has generated an extraordinary ramping up of compensatory violence, both real and symbolic. The film's detailed exploration of counterterrorism—including its depiction of torture and rendition, the secret raid on bin Laden's compound, and the umbrella of surveillance that has been imposed on global life—conveys the present historical moment in all its dark reality, while at the same time opening a space of imaginative projection, a space that I have described in terms of enchantment and disenchantment, haunting and exorcism. Jackson refers to a "permanent condition of 'waiting for terror'" in national and international life, and the "institutionalization of a politics of fear."[21] In *Zero Dark Thirty*, the pursuit and killing of bin Laden momentarily holds this condition at bay, while simultaneously bringing into view a parallel track of cultural projection, in which the violence of terror has penetrated the national imaginary and become an organizing cultural and historical fact.

CHAPTER 3

INTIMATE VIOLENCE

Drone Vision in *Eye in the Sky*

EYE IN THE SKY (2015) BRINGS INTO CRYSTALLIZED VIEW the tension between two dominant Western frameworks for representing and imagining war in the twenty-first century—the military dream of war waged at a distance with remote weaponry, emblematized in the seemingly godlike figure of the drone pilot hurling invisible thunderbolts from the sky; and the reality of the close, intimate violence of drone combat, where the existential and visceral struggles of war return in a new form. The film brings these two antithetical frameworks into close connection, conveying the instrumental power of networked war—its extraordinary technological resources and optical clarity—while at the same time detailing, and bringing home to the spectator, the psychological impact of close-up perspective and familiarity in the act of killing. *Eye in the Sky* dramatizes the radical overturning of tactical and ethical protocols for war under the influence of the drone, illuminating the way it has transformed traditional models of hostile and friendly territory and older concepts of the limits of force while at the same time suturing the audience to the perceptual and emotional perspective of the drone pilots, who watch the injury and death they unleash unfold on video screens eighteen inches away. In the film, the clichés of distanced warfare are swept away in the eyewitness experience of the drone pilots, whose acts of targeting, releasing the missiles, and visually analyzing the carnage below brings the experience that Yuval Noah Harari calls "flesh witnessing" into a strange new contemporary war setting.[1] As the journalist Mark Bowden writes, "Flying a drone, [the pilot] sees the carnage close-up, in real time. . . . Often he's been watching the people he kills for a long time before pulling the trigger."[2]

In the pages that follow, I consider the film's depiction of a fraught mission that brings into relief the new frames, practices, and consequences of drone warfare, dramatizing the moral crises and the losses of innocent life that shadow the technological forms of networked warfare. Detailing the elaborate procedural and interdepartmental calculus necessary to authorize a drone strike, the film poses a contemporary, real-world enactment of the well-known thought experiment known as the trolley problem, in which the subject must decide whether to sacrifice one person to save a larger number. As the military plan for the drone strike becomes entangled in political, legal, and public relations issues, moral questions of death, life, and what is permissible in war are thrust into the foreground. At the height of the film's escalating drama, the two young drone pilots are faced with an existential decision. They have been ordered to release a missile, targeting a well-known terrorist and her crew, including two suicide bombers, a strike that will almost certainly kill an innocent bystander—a young neighborhood girl whose daily life we have been following throughout the film. *Eye in the Sky* underscores the human costs—and the limits—of instrumentalized violence, even in political and military settings where advanced weapons systems have been enshrined.

The film unfolds over the course of a day. Crosscutting among four principal locations, *Eye in the Sky* details the complex coordination among multiple agencies (stretching from the UK, to Kenya, Nevada, and Hawaii) who work together to authorize and execute the drone strike dramatized in the film. A high-ranking terrorist, a British national, is the target of the strike; she has been tracked to a neighborhood hideout in Nairobi, where the British military, with help from Kenyan soldiers, hopes to capture her, and if they cannot, to target her with a missile carried by a U.S.-controlled Reaper drone high in the sky. Linked by satellite phone and live video feeds, the "kill chain" involved in the drone strike consists of military units in both the UK and the United States, and a disparate group of UK politicians, cabinet ministers, and lawyers who must authorize the strike. A Kenyan military unit on the ground waits in support. The film provides a close exposition of the political, legal, and military issues that the strike entails, an unwieldy congeries that results in multiple points of disagreement and internal conflict. When a young neighborhood girl, Alia (Aisha Takow), walks directly into the blast zone and sits at a table to sell the bread her mother has made, the decision of whether to strike the target becomes a desperate exercise in working out what Eyal Weizman, after Hannah Arendt, calls "the logic of the lesser evil."[3]

THE VERTICALIZATION OF POWER

The representation of contested space constitutes one of the fundamental genre codes of war cinema, a genre in which geopolitics serves a paramount narrative role. In the cinema of war, as in the prosecution of actual war, ordinary places such as fields, shorelines, forests, and cities are charged with significance, transformed into hostile and friendly zones, battlefronts, perimeters, and no-man's-lands. Central to this spatial orientation is the idea of the battle zone as a space of exception, where violence is the norm and the weapons of war are as much a part of the mise-en-scène as the landscape itself. Demarcated from the battle zone, however, are areas that are ordinarily regarded as outside the purview of military action, civilian zones that serve as refuges, safe from attack. The vertical spaces of drone combat, however, necessarily redefine this fundamental genre code; the practices of drone warfare assume a borderless, deterritorialized battle space, not limited by older concepts of geography. The verticalization of power produces its own claims to sovereignty. As Grégoire Chamayou says, "The aerial weapon . . . draws its own lines in the sky."[4] Moreover, the reach of vertical power is not limited to a particular field of engagement: it can be deployed anywhere the global war on terror seems to demand the use of the aerial weapon. Chamayou continues by pointing out that the goal of the dominant power is no longer to occupy territory but to control it, indefinitely, from above: "We are entering a world of winged and armed panoptics."[5] In *Eye in the Sky,* this new concept of the battle space is set forth in a particularly concentrated way.

Opening with an intimate family scene in Nairobi, the film begins by conveying a sense of domesticity and familiarity, as a working-class father is shown making a colorful Hula-Hoop for his ten-year-old daughter, Alia. Accompanied by minor-key, traditional stringed music, the camera begins to move through the family setting, gradually widening and lifting its view to an overhead shot of the family courtyard. As the camera begins to climb to a higher position, however, the music changes to deep brass and drums, as we take in the surrounding neighborhood. The shot then focuses on a jeep filled with armed men patrolling the streets. A set of crosshairs is superimposed on the jeep, transforming the overhead view into a targeting operation. The title of the film, *Eye in the Sky*, emerges from the crosshairs and is displayed across the screen, as the shot widens to encompass the outlying neighborhoods of Nairobi and the skyscrapers of the city beyond.

In this opening, the theme of ubiquitous, continuous surveillance, of control from above, is enunciated in the film's initial shots. The jeep is itself subject to the aerial patrol from above. And as the crosshairs are fixed on the vehicle, a zone of armed conflict is opened, one that is not defined by geocentric concepts of battlefront or hostile territory, but rather by the location of the target—in Chamayou's terms, a target-centered conflict zone that is "attached to the bodies of the enemy–prey."[6]

In war cinema, the panorama shot, usually from an aerial perspective, is a nearly ubiquitous device, a topographic orientation to the space in which the violence of combat will unfold. Providing a sense of both optical power and immersion—the beginnings of the helicopter raid sequence in *Apocalypse Now* (1979) is an example—the aerial panorama shot is often a heightened, sensuous moment of pure cinema. In the opening shots of *Eye in the Sky*, however, the optical overview communicates something else. Rather than marking an aesthetic overture or dramatic prelude, the beginning of *Eye in the Sky* conveys a weaponized optics of surveillance and targeting—of control from above. Far from the "destructive sublime" that one writer finds in the aerial shots of World War II films,[7] or the aesthetic plenitude that many modernist writers described in the early years of flight, aerial vision here exemplifies what Harun Farocki calls "operative images," a form of sighting whose goal is not to represent persons, objects, or the contours of the landscape, but to act on them, to target them.[8] The visual codes that had once defined aerial vision as a new mode of modernist perception, a perspective signifying aesthetic renewal and embodied freedom have been converted to the instrumental mechanisms of surveillance and control.[9]

COMBAT AS HUNTING

In the first act, the film details the complex networks of distributed warfare that characterize drone operation in the current period, depicting several military, political, legal, and undercover agents in different locations, linked by video emanating from the U.S. drone, the "eye in the sky." A terrorist leader, Susan Danford (Lex King)—a subject of surveillance for years—has been tracked to Nairobi, and a British military anti-terror unit headed by Lieutenant General Frank Benson (Alan Rickman) and Colonel Katherine Powell (Helen Mirren), operating from separate locations in the UK, has enlisted the U.S. military in the drone surveillance of the target. The mission, at this point in the film, is to capture Danford. In addition to the British military command, the mission involves a Kenyan military unit in Nairobi ready to dispatch to Danford's hideout; two drone pilots and their support team located at Creech Air Base in the Nevada desert; a team of facial recognition analysts in position in Hawaii; and a ground-level, undercover agent, Jama Farah (Barkhad Abdi), in Nairobi. Also part of the network, on the British side, are a cabinet minister, a lawyer for the British government, and an observer from the British Parliament. Nearly all the team members are distributed in secure locations distant from Nairobi, with the exception of the Kenyan undercover operative, who controls two miniature surveillance drones—a mechanical, helicopter bird and a flying beetle that will prove critical to the mission.

The film's depiction of the coordinated surveillance and pursuit across three continents in exact, second-by-second communication illuminates a decisive turn in the practices of war and in the ways it is imagined—from the paradigm of combat to the paradigm of hunting. While combat occurs when opposing forces clash in a space demarcated by fronts, lines, and areas of territorial control, hunting occurs wherever the prey goes. The enemy, in this scenario, carries with it its "own little mobile zone of hostility." The enemy can be tracked and pursued anywhere, regardless of notions of territorial sovereignty. In Chamayou's words, "What is emerging is the idea of an invasive power based not so much on the rights of conquest as on the rights of pursuit: a right of universal incursion or encroachment."[10] *Eye in the Sky* brings this change into dramatic focus, as the conventions of the attack and the assault—what Garrett Stewart has called "the choreographed and panoramic staples of the combat genre, beachheads to be won, fortresses held"—have disappeared.[11] Once a fundamental topos of drama and meaning in the war film, combat has now metamorphosed into the radically different patterns of hunting and pursuit. In place of agonistic physical struggle, the dramatic emphasis has now shifted to a paradigm based on the hunt.

One of the most interesting by-products of the drone-hunting paradigm is the development of the concept of "kill boxes," a way of extending the legal–spatial definition of the armed conflict zone, in which certain types of military actions and weapons of war are permitted, to spaces outside the geocentric definition of the battlefield. A kill box or a "kill cube," for example, might be opened in a house in an otherwise peaceful neighborhood, or even in a single room of an apartment in a "friendly" city. For the proponents of mobile antiterrorist pursuit, a kill box is a temporary expedient, a free-fire zone that can be closed down as soon as the armed action is finished. It can also be miniaturized, reduced to the physical body of the enemy: the body of the enemy now becomes the battlefield.[12] As Derek Gregory writes, "The target is contracted to the individual human body even as the field of military violence expands to encompass the globe."[13]

In *Eye in the Sky,* the procedures and protocols of drone targeting are detailed in a series of dramatic plot turns and high-level, urgent exchanges among the command-and-control teams in the United States and Great Britain. The primary subjects of surveillance in Nairobi, the terrorist Susan Danford and her husband—numbers 2 and 5 on the U.S. State Department's most wanted list—have surprised the surveillance team by moving from the location where they had been expected to stay to a stronghold controlled by the terrorist group al-Shabaab. The plan for a military capture of Danford now proves to be impossible—a military-style incursion into that heavily protected neighborhood would lead to a certain massacre. An alternative plan is quickly proposed by Colonel Powell: obtain a positive ID of Danford and attack the compound immediately with the Hellfire missiles

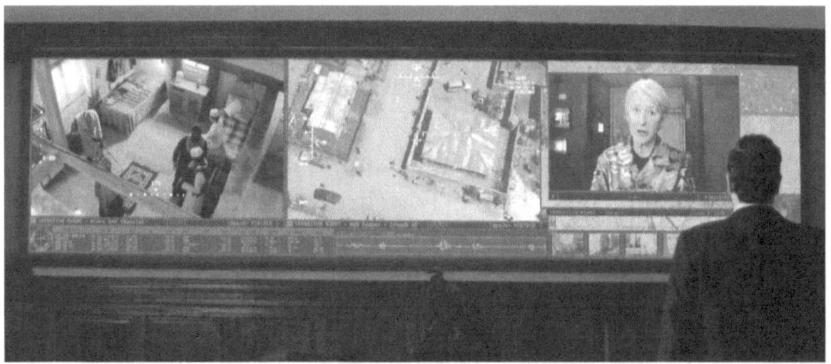

Split-screen image of Colonel Powell, making the case for a drone strike on the house containing several terrorists. *Eye in the Sky,* directed by Gavin Hood, 2015. Produced by Ged Doherty, Colin Firth, and David Lancaster.

mounted on the Reaper drone circling above, killing Danford, her husband, and the other terrorists in the house.

First, however, a positive identification of Danford must be made. Jama, the Kenyan agent on the ground, maneuvers a tiny robot in the form of a flying beetle—a "surveillance micro air vehicle" as one writer calls it—into the house. After Danford's ID is confirmed, Colonel Powell immediately asks permission to open a kill box—declaring that the mere presence of the two terrorists is sufficient to authorize a strike. The rules of war that apply to this new definition of the conflict zone are explicitly evoked here: wherever the two terrorists go, the weapons of war can be employed against them. The body of the terrorist carries its own mobile conflict zone with it—the body becomes the battlefield.

Colonel Powell pursues the female terrorist Danford with a cool and professional focus that bears certain similarities to the character of Maya in *Zero Dark Thirty* (2012). Powell, like Maya, eschews any form of what is conventionally understood to be gendered behavior. Although she is the only female soldier in her drone tracking unit, and the male British soldiers that she commands routinely address her as "ma'am"—which sounds like "mum" when they pronounce it—there is no hint of gendered inflection in her style of command, nor in the male soldiers' behavior toward her. But where Maya's authority in *Zero Dark Thirty* comes from her implacable and even frightening conviction that she, alone, has discovered the key to locating bin Laden, and that she alone can bring about his execution,

Powell carries a different air: that of a well-seasoned professional motivated to take Danford out of circulation mainly for reasons of military and state necessity.

It is of interest, however, that the film, at its core, revolves around four female characters: Colonel Powell, the terrorist Susan Danford, the young Kenyan girl Alia, and the parliamentary observer Angela Northman (Monica Dolan), who insistently questions the mission's legality and ethics. In what is clearly an unprecedented move in the history of the war film, the major actants of the narrative—the figures who push the plot forward and are responsible both for the narrative's twists and turns and, in the case of Northman, for attempting to reset the agenda—are all female characters. This surprising importance is somewhat camouflaged by the prominence of Lieutenant General Benson in the story as well as the drone pilot, Lieutenant Steve Watts (Aaron Paul). The male characters, however, function mainly as relays, communicating different perspectives on the attack, or following orders. On the structural level of plot events, changes in plot direction, and the arrival at a resolution, the female characters control the levers of narrative.

The positive identification of Danford and her husband in the Nairobi hideout sets in motion a series of legal, moral, and political debates that illuminate the radical shifts in military practice and protocol that have emerged with the new weaponry of the drone. Detailing the kill chain of drone pilots, military commanders, data analysts, facial recognition experts, government ministers, lawyers, and members of Parliament that are called on to authorize and implement the strike, the film underlines the fact that a drone attack in the new battle space of twenty-first-century war must be weighed as much for its political consequences as for its military value.

Giving full voice to the military case for removing the terrorists, the film also depicts an extraordinary effort to provide judicial and political justification for the strike. In contrast to the unambiguous stance of the military officers calling for the strike, the cabinet minister and the lawyer for the British government engage in a series of equivocations, hedging their political risk, sidestepping responsibility, and insisting on "referring up." Rather than the split-second decisions that combat in the field entails, the decision to commit to a drone strike is portrayed as fraught with political calculation, where the rules of engagement are shaped to a great degree by potential political blowback and bad publicity.

Against this new, emergent logic of postheroic war—war waged at a distance, without physical risk to the soldiers fighting it—the film provides a counterargument, voiced through Northman, the skeptical parliamentary observer. Restating an older understanding of the armed conflict zone, she insists that the mission authorized only the capture of Danford, not her assassination. Moreover, she asserts an older spatial paradigm of war, where national borders divide hostile from allied territories: "Has there ever been a British-led drone attack on a city in a friendly country that is not at war?" The debate that follows between the proponents of drone hunting, where the rights of pursuit and encroachment supersede the sovereign rights of bordered nations, and the advocates of more traditional military rules of engagement, is ratcheted up with every turn in the drama. And with each new development, the traditional codes of war—and the genre codes of the war film—are confronted by a new framing of the tactics and ethics of combat emblematized in the drone.

THE APPARATUS

Expanding on the long-standing association of drones and weaponized vision first theorized by Paul Virilio, Derek Gregory provides a surprising description of the cultural technology of the drone that emphasizes the subjective effects of drone warfare, comparing the kill chain to the workings of the cinematic apparatus theorized in the work of Christian Metz and Jean-Louis Baudry. As in the theory of the apparatus, the subjectivity of the participants—the pilots, technicians, and commanders involved in the operation of the drone—serves as a crucial part of the functioning of its optical system: "The kill-chain can be thought of as a dispersed and distributed apparatus, a congeries of actors, objects, practices, discourses and affects, that entrains the people who are made part of it and constitutes them as particular kinds of subjects."[14] The images and viewing positions of drone warfare shape the subjectivity not only of drone pilots, he argues, but of everyone involved in the operation. Because of the intimacy of drone imagery, everyone in the kill chain network, he concludes, is brought much closer to the "killing space."[15]

The film thus instantiates a turn away from the cold technology of what once constituted "virtual" war—the kind of war at a distance defined by the laser-guided missiles of the Gulf War—to a new paradigm of intimate violence rendered through enhanced optical technology—a new kind of "somatic witnessing."[16] The visibilities of contemporary drone warfare, Gregory explains, "produce a special kind of intimacy that consistently privileges the view of the hunter–killer."[17]

The view of the hunter–killer, connected in intimate optical relation to the potential and actual victims of violence, is explored in detail in the film. In each of the several command-and-control centers, large-scale, close-up views of the targets are displayed on vivid, wall-sized screens, underlining optical privilege as well as intimacy that produces its own coded styles of looking. Although the members of the separate command teams are invisible to one another, communicating over secure audio transmissions and telephones, the terror suspects, the house where they are situated, and the neighborhood that surrounds it are represented in a multiscreen display in each location, compulsively reiterated with every crosscut from one control center to the other.

INTIMATE VIOLENCE

In the closing third of the film, however, *Eye in the Sky* turns the military optics of drone technology back on the agents of the gaze. In the film's third act, the decision to strike or to stand down hinges on the question of "collateral damage," as Alia sets up her bread stand directly outside the wall of the target house. From this point forward, Alia provides the work's dramatic fulcrum; her fate becomes the subject of an ethical and political debate that ricochets from one command center to another. Like the giant, real-life photo of a little girl created by an activist team in Pakistan to confront drone pilots surveilling their village, *Eye in the Sky* sets the imagined life of one little girl against an immense system of technologized warfare.[18]

The discovery that two of the terrorists are preparing for an imminent suicide attack, and are being outfitted with suicide vests and making a suicide video inside the house, makes the decision to strike a matter of extreme urgency: once they escape the target house and move out into the crowded neighborhood, or perhaps to a mall, they will be impossible to strike and will present a grave danger to the civilian population. Although the decision to strike has been buttressed by this new information, the appearance of Alia in the kill zone moments before the Hellfire missile is to be released changes the calculation. The close-up intimacy the film has established with Alia gives her character a substantial human presence, an existential weight, providing a counterbalance to the strict military calculus that would consider her almost-certain death an acceptable cost of war. And in the diegetic micro-drama played out here, the optical intimacy afforded by the drone—as every member of the kill chain is confronted by close-ups of her from the eye in the sky above—seems to shift the balance in the ethics of violence, temporarily halting the attack.

The pilot, from his secure location in Nevada, zooms in on Alia; realizing that he and his copilot had noticed her earlier while she was playing with her hoop in her yard, he refuses to release the missile and requests a new estimate of collateral damage. Countermanding the direct and increasingly insistent order from Colonel Powell in the UK to execute the mission, the drone pilot asserts his authority as commander of the aircraft and places the missile in disarmed mode, pending a new estimate of the risk to the young girl.

THE ETHICS OF NETWORKED WAR

With this scene, the film counterposes two distinct philosophies of war. Although it presents the verticalization of power as a fully operational and accepted doctrine, where an aboveground authority is empowered to police and destroy any street, house, or person within it, the film retains, in vestigial form, the genre memory of the rescue narrative and the duty to protect the noncombatant—a residue of the past embedded in the generic DNA of the war film. The codes of military honor that are retained by the drone pilots cut against the emergent hunter–killer paradigm as the overarching doctrine of contemporary war. In *Eye in the Sky,* this older code of honor remains as a kernel of resistance within the military hierarchy and is directly expressed in the refusal of the drone pilot tasked with releasing the weapon. As the film details the pilot's hand on the trigger, his sweating, uncertain facial expressions, his sideways glances at his copilot, vertical war suddenly assumes an intimate, personal character. The act of killing from afar has become a visceral and life-defining event.

Two antithetical scripts are thus superimposed on the drone pilots in *Eye in the Sky;* they are suspended between two very different moral worlds, pulled between an older narrative of war that hinges on the duty to protect and an emerging doctrine of risk transfer, where all danger is shifted away from the soldier and onto the civilian population. For several minutes in the film, the optical apparatus of the drone awakens in the pilots this older military code, which predates and supersedes the orders they are given by their commanders.

The historian Yuval Noah Harari has argued that the cultural history of war since the military period has been dominated by three conceptions: war as instrumental, leading to an improvement in collective or individual life; war as honorary, a worthwhile endeavor in its own right; and war as revelation, either positive or negative, expressing the ultimate truth of the self and the world. Since the early twentieth-century, the concept of war as revelation—an experience that exposes the truth of the self and the world—has dominated the cultural understanding and image of war, with the literature, films, and memoires of World War I, World War II, and Vietnam often pervaded by themes of negative revelation, disillusionment, and trauma. As Harari writes, the experience of war is seen as a kind of ultimate truth that only those who have experienced it "in the flesh" can understand.[19]

In the twenty-first century, however, the pervasive idea of war at a distance has blurred the formerly unbridgeable divide between those who experience war firsthand and those whose knowledge of war is mediated by technology. With command decisions often made from remote locations—the drone pilots' trailers in the Nevada desert, for example, or Western command centers secreted in suburban settings—war is often experienced primarily through media networks, through screens and optical devices—in other words, through digital mediation. As a consequence, the gulf between the physical experience of battle and the technologically mediated representation of war appears to have been overridden. What follows, for many writers, is a sense that war—and the war film—has shifted to a "battle of the screens" blanketed in digital media, with the truth of war—and in the case of the war film, its narrative power—essentially obviated.[20]

The drone pilot Lieutenant Watts after the missile has been released. *Eye in the Sky,* directed by Gavin Hood, 2015. Produced by Ged Doherty, Colin Firth, and David Lancaster.

In the drone strike portrayed in *Eye in the Sky,* however, the existential meaning of remote combat is brought into relief. Moreover, it is the optical technology of the drone, the primary weapon of wars conducted at a distance, that brings home the costs of war. What Harari calls "flesh witnessing" is plainly expressed in the heightened emotion of the pilots, agonizing over the decision to strike, as well as the other members of the kill chain, scrutinizing the screen and searching for a decision or a mechanism that will spare the little girl while still killing the terrorists.

The film's focus on the pilots' dilemma, however, also creates a surprising reversal, as the pathos of war and sacrifice now shifts from the victims of war to its agents. Oblivious to the threat from above, unaware of the fact that her tiniest gestures are being watched on screens on three different continents and in at least three locations, ignorant of the fateful decision now being made from afar, Alia is placed, at this crucial juncture, in the role of almost-certain tragic victim. However, in a critical twist, the pathos associated with sacrifice and death in war is transferred from Alia to the pilots who are tasked with carrying out the order to strike. Rather than the singular subject of pathos, she serves as a kind of lever for maximizing emotion, both in the pilots and in the audience, emotions that are familiar from the long history of war films. In a way that is similar to other films in this study, including *A Private War, Restrepo,* and *The Hurt Locker,* pathos is transferred from the persons who are the direct targets and victims of war to the white Westerners who are vested with agency and authority.

AN ENCHANTED WEAPON

Certain war theorists have called the drone a "moral weapon," one that protects both soldiers and innocents, a "humanitarian weapon" that causes less collateral damage than the mass bombing campaigns of the past. Elevated to an almost magical status by its proponents, the drone is conceived as a power that, in the words of Chamayou, "both kills and saves, wounds and heals," and it performs these double tasks in a single, integrated gesture: "an immediate synthesis of a power of destruction and a power of caring."[21]

For the proponents of the hunter drone, the Reaper and the Predator are seen as transformative, a technology allowing an almost limitless power of attack. Moreover, the attack need not be actualized. Hovering out of sight, the drone creates a sense of constant threat, producing an intense and continuous anxiety in the target population. As Lisa Parks writes, "Drones may sidestep the dirty work of torture, but they advance other kinds of psychological operations, using the sky to delineate and administer zones of surveillance and fear, death and destruction."[22] And the violence the drone causes is somewhat sanitized. As Gregory describes it, the public is "no longer confronted by images of the widespread destruction caused by the area bombing of cities or the carpet bombing of villages in the rainforest."[23] Instead, discrete strikes on individual buildings or vehicles leave the surrounding structures intact.

Furthering the idea of the drone as an enchanted weapon, the drone interface bears no physical marks—the drone lens is never spattered with blood or flesh, and its imagery arrives on the screens of the pilots and members of the kill chain unaccompanied by sound, smell, or the concussive impact of physical proximity. Indeed, the absence of sound is particularly telling, as sound, in effect, shapes and colors the image. Nasser Hussain describes the absence of synchronic sound in drone combat in a particularly vivid way: the lack of sound "renders it a ghostly world in which the figures seem unalive, even before they are killed. The gaze hovers above in silence. The detachment that critics of drone operations worry about comes partially from the silence of the footage."[24]

None of these forms of detachment is available to the spectator of *Eye in the Sky.* Cutting between overhead views of the terror compound, with Alia sitting at her bread stand outside it, and ground-level cameras that give us direct shots of the girl, the pilot finally, after receiving a new collateral damage estimate from Colonel Powell, reluctantly releases the weapon. From this point, *Eye in the Sky* depicts the effects of drone warfare in a way that pulls the mask of magic from the technology of contemporary war. Depicting in vivid close-up and full panoramic sound the death and destruction caused by the drone attack, the film cuts together silent shots taken from the drone with footage from the ground, accompanied by sound, rendering fully the gruesome effects of the Hellfire missile, in a montage sequence anchored by repeated low-angle shots of Alia's wounded body. Framed through a scrim of fire and smoke in the foreground, the ground-level view of Alia lying prone and moving only her hands suggests the full portfolio of embodied experiences in war, including the heat, din, and general pandemonium of a shock attack. Violence here expresses not the cleansing erasure of the terrorist threat, Susan Danford, but the "bare, forked existence of the violated being," Alia.[25] Cutting back to the perspective of the drone pilots, the film also suggests the psychic wounding that drone warfare inflicts on the agents of war, the moral injury, plainly registered in the faces of the drone operators.

Stunned by what they have just unleashed, the pilots are ordered to inspect, in close-up, the carnage in the rubble of the house in order to identify the body parts, to make sure they have eliminated the target. Discovering that Danford is still alive, they are commanded to release a second missile, ensuring that Alia will be killed. The detailed camera work renders the effects of destruction in a way that emphasizes the visceral experience of war, placing us in imaginative proximity to the event, closing the gap between witnessing and experience.

THE LOGIC OF THE LESSER EVIL

In the concluding scenes of *Eye in the Sky,* the spectator is confronted, once again, with the central question that has reverberated throughout the film. The parliamentary observer, Northman, who had resisted the prosecution of the mission, initiates a tense exchange with

General Benson: "Never tell a soldier he does not know the cost of war." *Eye in the Sky*, directed by Gavin Hood, 2015. Produced by Ged Doherty, Colin Firth, and David Lancaster.

General Benson, who had been supervising the assault, reveals, in words, the high emotion that had been earlier expressed principally in the participants' body language—the clenched postures, the visible sweating, the defensive gestures. Departing from the controlled lexicon of legal and political deliberation, Northman protests that what they just did was "shameful." The pointed response by Benson is withering; he has seen firsthand the death and destruction caused by a suicide bomber, has walked among the bodies; while others may quibble about life and death over "coffee and biscuits," the soldier alone has seen behind the screen: "Never tell a soldier he does not know the cost of war," he concludes. His words recall, in pointed language, the chasm between those who have experienced war and those who have not, and implies a distinction between the visceral understanding acquired on the actual battlefield and the experience of mediated war—a distinction the film had appeared to dissolve.

Eyal Weizman calls the type of justification Benson makes "the logic of the lesser evil," arguing that it is "the essence of our humanitarian present, obsessed with the calculations and calibrations that seek to moderate, ever so slightly, the evils it has largely caused itself."[26] General Benson accepts the incidental killing of Alia as a straightforward example of the "lesser evil." Faced with the much greater destruction that would likely be caused by the two suicide bombers, as well as the untold future carnage that Susan Danford and her terror group would wreak if she were to escape, Benson asserts, implicitly, that the sacrifice of one civilian life is justified,

Alia, the young victim of "collateral damage" from the drone attack. *Eye in the Sky*, directed by Gavin Hood, 2015. Produced by Ged Doherty, Colin Firth, and David Lancaster.

that "collateral damage" is an acceptable cost of war. However, as Weizman further explains concerning the "cumulativeness" of lesser evils, "Even according to the terms of an economy of losses and gains, the concept of the lesser evil risks becoming counterproductive: less brutal methods are also those that may be more easily naturalized, accepted and tolerated—and hence more frequently used, with the result that a greater evil may be reached cumulatively."[27] The film suggests that "lesser" acts of state violence have become naturalized, inserted into the ordinary rhythm of quotidian domestic life.

No such logic of the lesser evil mitigates the harm to Alia, her family, and her neighbors. In the film's final scene, as Alia's broken body is placed on the very jeep we had viewed from the perspective of the drone in the opening sequence, its gun thrown out to make room for the injured girl, the film's larger message comes through. Rushed to the hospital and through its hallways, Alia is quickly attended to by the emergency room staff. When the doctor shakes his head and her father and mother perceive the gesture, the impact of her death seems to override General Benson's words about the cost of war. And in the closing credit sequence of the film, we are presented with a coda, a flashback scene of Alia, alive and smiling, twirling her hoop in the family yard, leaving us with an image that brings the full tragedy of her death into view and puts the spectator's own act of witnessing—and judgment—squarely in the frame.

CHAPTER 4

WAR AS REVELATION

A Private War

THE STORY OF THE CELEBRATED WAR CORRESPONDENT Marie Colvin (played by Rosamund Pike), *A Private War* (2018) takes a very different approach to representing war than the films I have previously considered in this volume. Its protagonist, a conflict journalist, is not a soldier of any army or an agent of any state. She wields no weapons, nor does she follow orders or issue commands. Nevertheless, she has "seen more war than most soldiers," as one her colleagues remarks, and is targeted for execution by a state military. Exploring an aspect of contemporary war that has seldom been represented fully in film, *A Private War* dramatizes Colvin's experiences on the front lines of multiple conflicts, portraying the hidden reality of today's warfare as an unending series of grotesque assaults on civilian populations, often conducted by governments against their own people, with women and children the primary targets and victims. In scene after scene, the emblematic imagery of war—the devastated cities, the corpses on the roadside, the shell bursts and weapons' fire—signifies not the pitched struggle of armies or irregular soldiers in combat with one another, but the ravaging of ordinary people.

The film follows the last ten years of Colvin's life, from the time of her blinding in one eye in Sri Lanka in 2001 to her death in Homs, Syria, in 2012, where she was targeted and killed by the Syrian military. Focusing on both her courage and determination on the front lines of conflict and on her difficult personal life between assignments, *A Private War* portrays Colvin as a journalist committed to giving voice to the civilian victims of war, but also as a character periodically lost to cycles of traumatic memory and alcoholism. The events the film dramatizes are drawn from the dozens of brutal conflicts that Colvin reported on during this period, both in well-known war zones and in places where undeclared civil wars or insurrections were underway. Throughout the film, scenes set in harrowing conflict zones are juxtaposed with sequences set in London, where Colvin's life is depicted as replete with parties, gala celebrations of her award-winning journalism, and the terrors of nightmarish memories. From this decade-long carousel of violence and trauma, the film concentrates on her reporting in several specific locations—Sri Lanka, Iraq, Palestine, Libya, Syria—emphasizing her concentrated focus on the innocent victims of war, the main theme in her reporting. As the real-life Colvin has written, "Despite all the videos you see on television, what's on the ground has remained remarkably the same for the past 100 years. Craters. Burnt houses. Women weeping for sons and daughters. . . . War is not clean. War is about those who are killed, limbs severed, dirt and rock and flesh torn alike by hot metal. It is terror. It is mothers, fathers, sons and daughters bereft and inconsolable. It is about traumatised children."[1]

As the film proceeds, Colvin's headline stories about the deliberate targeting of civilians as a tactic of war makes her a target in her own right, an aspect of contemporary war—the intentional killing of journalists—that marks a striking change from the past. This turn in the conventions and codes of the battlefield is suggested in the film's initial scene. As *A Private War* opens, we hear Colvin's voice on the soundtrack, part of an interview she conducted late in her career, reluctantly responding to a question about feeling fear when on assignment: "It feels like I am writing my own obituary," she says, allowing that "fear comes later, when it is all over." The camera is positioned at an overhead angle, looking directly down on a bombed-out building, as her voice over continues. Across the middle of the shot, a graphic title informs us that this is the city of Homs, Syria. As the camera begins tracking upward and back, it brings into view a city that has been shelled into rubble, the muted brown and rust colors of the place already merging with the colors of the desert that surrounds it. Three sets of legs can be seen lying inert under the broken concrete. As the voice of Colvin continues on the soundtrack, the camera begins to tilt toward the horizon, depicting a landscape defined by smoking ruins. At the end of the film, we return to this shot and to the interview: it is the scene of Colvin's death, an overture of sorts that is also a final curtain, foregrounding the attacks on civilians—and journalists—that will form a central topic of the film.

In this chapter, I consider *A Private War* as equal parts biopic and war film, exploring the ways the film stretches the contours of both genres. The characteristic structural forms of the war film—for example, including the straightforward, linear chronology that is typical of the genre, its geographic concentration to a few, concrete locales, as well as its rhythmic patterns of intense struggle followed by periods of quiet waiting—are missing from *A Private War*, which has a complicated time scheme and features frequent changes of setting. Missing too, however, are the cardinal features of the biopic, with its plots typically organized around the struggle for artistic, scientific, or other forms of public success against a backdrop of adversity and skepticism. As *A Private War* begins, Colvin is already at the pinnacle of her career. Moreover, with a woman at the center of the film, the genre codes of both the biopic and the war film are torqued in an even more pronounced fashion, as both genres have served, historically, as vehicles of male drama. The film stands apart even from its direct antecedents, films in which the biopic and the war film converge—a small but distinguished group of works that includes *Patton* (1970), *Schindler's List* (1993), *Lawrence of Arabia*, (1962), and *Born on the Fourth of July* (1989)—works that have been celebrated as exemplary studies of masculinity in the crisis of wartime.[2]

Nevertheless, the film engages in a powerful and important way with themes that I have identified in this volume as core, fundamental subjects of war cinema—the late modern idea of war as truth, the truth of the self and the world, which can only be had through direct, first-person experience. In *A Private War*, Colvin's insistence on "seeing it for myself," her repeated refrain "Once you've seen, once you've seen," and her statement to her editor that "I see it so that you don't have to" is asserted both as a necessary and distinguishing component of her reportage of war, and critiqued as a form of pathology, an addiction to risk.

"MY JOB IS TO BEAR WITNESS"

Following the overture, the film begins with a scene in London, where Colvin is seen lying in bed, smoking, and talking with her former husband (Greg Wise), who reminds her that she is "not thirty-five anymore." We then cut to the London offices of the *Sunday Times*, where the camera finds Colvin stalking the workspace and struggling with her computer. Over the course of the film, the tension between Colvin's extreme commitment to her field assignments and her acute sense of dislocation and frustration in the domestic settings of London is made manifest. Already a celebrity for her front-line dispatches, Colvin is here depicted resisting pressure to move into an editorial role with the newspaper; she insists to her editor that she be allowed to follow up on a lead and make her way into the deep jungle region controlled by the Tamil Tigers in Sri Lanka. Although the Sri Lankan government had isolated the region, and barred all outside contact, Colvin enters the camp by stealth and succeeds in interviewing the second in command of the rebel forces. There, she discovers that the government has blocked international aid sent to the region, essentially starving the civilian population in the area under dispute. She is shown into a tent city where thousands of hungry women and children have been gathered. Colvin's own account placed the number at 340,000 refugees.[3]

As Colvin and her small escort party attempt to leave the rebel territory, winding their way through the jungle at night, they encounter a patrol of government troops, who spot them and begin shooting. Taking cover, she quickly realizes that the soldiers will almost certainly discover her. Standing up to identify herself, Colvin shouts that she is unarmed, a journalist, and an American. Immediately, a rocket-propelled grenade is fired at her, an assault that results in Colvin being wounded by shrapnel in several places, including her left eye. In the hospital, she is told that her eye has been irreparably damaged and that sight in that eye is gone.

The wounding of the protagonist in the first full scene of the film orients the narrative around trauma, violence, and suffering—Colvin is no sooner introduced than she receives a disfiguring wound—underlining the role of what Yuval Noah Harari calls flesh witnessing

Marie Colvin, attacked by soldiers in Sri Lanka, despite her shouting that she is a journalist. *A Private War*, directed by Mark Heineman, 2018. Produced by Matthew George, Mark Heineman, Basil Iwanyk, Marissa McMahon, and Charlize Theron.

in contemporary representations of war. With the wounded eye serving as the film's primary symbol and index of risk, Colvin's injury—and the signature eye patch that she wears to conceal it—confers a kind of aura on the character, as if she has acquired access to a privileged zone of truth. Harari describes flesh witnessing in the following way: "What is it about war that reveals truth? Most late-modern veterans point to the extreme bodily conditions of war: hunger, cold, exhaustion, injury, the presence of death—and occasionally the thrill of killing and the exhilarating adrenalin rush of combat . . . veterans lay claim to the visceral authority of 'flesh-witnessing' . . . they are men (and occasionally women) who have learned their wisdom with their flesh."[4]

Colvin's insistence on "seeing it for myself" crystallizes the themes Harari explores and brings a new dimension into view. As a journalist, however, Colvin is charged with forming a bridge of words between those who have witnessed the horrors of war directly and those who have not. In Harari's view, this is an impossible task: "Those who were not there cannot understand it . . . it is impossible to describe . . . a flesh witness cannot really describe what she witnessed, and the audience cannot really understand."[5] Nevertheless, Colvin repeatedly asserts that this is the most important role of conflict journalism. The recurrent scenes of trauma that flash into Colvin's mind screen as she is trying to sleep, or sometimes when composing her copy, might be read as the film's attempt to dramatize the costs of this impossible demand, as if her writing had to be grounded in the flesh memory and experience of suffering in order to be genuine. In a sense, the suffering of others must be converted into her own. Her efforts to bear witness, her insistence on seeing it for herself in order to serve as a direct conduit of emotion and embodied knowledge to the public, using words as her medium, trigger a nightmarish reiteration of traumatic scenes, where the suffering of others becomes vividly hers.

The concept of flesh witnessing, of war as revealing the truth of the self and the world, has a long-standing imprimatur in male-focused war films, which frequently revolve around the moment when the male soldier is transformed by war experience. Examples run throughout the history of the genre, with particularly noteworthy examples in films such as *Saving Private Ryan* (1998), *Full Metal Jacket* (1987), and *Flags of Our Fathers* (2006). Because representations of women's experience in war, however, have seldom touched on this important dimension, the opportunities to explore the heightened emotion and psychological shifts that flesh witnessing, in Harari's formulation, brings about have not been available. In the films in this study that feature female soldiers, such as *Zero Dark Thirty* (2012) and *Eye in the Sky* (2015), the women protagonists are physically distant from the battle space, although they are foregrounded as the agents in charge and are fully involved in the hands-on, existential, life-and-death dramas that the films present. In *A Private War*, however, the main character insists on being physically present, on experiencing war's conflict with her own flesh and her own senses. Like the characters of Sergeant William James of *The Hurt Locker* (2008) or Petty Officer Chris Kyle of *American Sniper* (2014), Colvin provides a cardinal example of productive pathology, putting herself, repeatedly, at extreme risk, seemingly addicted to the adrenalin of combat, in order to get the stories that no one else can. Unlike James or Kyle, however, her breakthrough moments must be captured in her prose, in the narration of what she has witnessed, in the communication of her experience, an experience that remains, almost by definition, incommunicable.

The mind- and body-altering experiences of combat that Colvin returns to repeatedly in the film depart in other ways, as well, from the male dramas of flesh witnessing that pervade the genre. The subject of her work, the civilian victims of war, in particular the women and children, are seldom represented in male-driven war narratives except as an anonymous multitude of the suffering. Yet even as it depicts the tragic effects of war on civilians, the film foregrounds Colvin, shifting, in a kind of rack focus, between the terror and agony experienced by the innocent victims and the traumatic experiences of Colvin herself. The pathos and loss the film depicts is channeled through the Western protagonist, a variant of the displacement of affect that I have discovered in several films I consider in this volume.

UNSPEAKABLE HISTORIES?

The film's representation of historical atrocity, what the film scholar William Guynn insightfully calls "unspeakable histories," brings this displacement into relief.[6] Directly after her recuperation in the hospital from the injury to her eye, Colvin returns to the field to cover the preparations for the United States invasion of Iraq. She and her photographer, Paul Conroy (Jamie Dornan), bluff their way into the interior of the country, sidestepping the U.S. pool program for embedding journalists, to pursue a tip from an informant about a mass grave filled with Saddam Hussein's victims. Upon arriving at the site Colvin hires a backhoe and directs the machine operator where to begin digging. As the scene unfolds, the excavation site is quickly surrounded by a number of Iraqis, male and female, holding pictures of loved ones and manifesting a growing sense of expectation. As the mechanical digger begins uncovering skulls, other bones, and bits of clothing, the black-robed women surrounding the pit begin to wail. And as the bodies are brought out and laid in orderly rows along the side, a powerful sense of documentary reality is produced, as the lamentations and gestures of the women communicate a deep sense of authenticity. The filmmaker, Matthew Heineman, has said that the Iraqi extras hired for this scene were in fact actual victims of Hussein's wars, although in reality the corpses buried at this location, as reported in Colvin's original published story, were Kuwaitis who had been captured by the Iraqi president in 1990. As Heineman says, "The women in that scene were Iraqi women crying about real trauma that they experienced, and at the end of that scene, like in any documentary that I made, something unforeseen happened: They started chanting and doing this prayer for the dead."[7]

Cutting between the black-robed women and shots of Colvin in close-up, smoking, with tears streaking her face, the film seems to be searching for a visual language to communicate the stark horror of the scene. Dozens of mass graves, containing tens of thousands of victims, were discovered in Hussein's Iraq, a historical record of mass murder that is condensed here into a singular expression of pathos and grief. But the personal trauma of the Western protagonist is also registered, as the film insistently keeps Colvin at the center. The foregrounding of Colvin in this sequence produces a complicated kind of signal noise, as if two contradictory frequencies were competing for space. To some extent, the repeated close-up shots of Colvin frame her as an authorizing figure, the symbolic and focal prism through which we view the events. The biographical Colvin, who discovered the grave and authored the story about it, is evoked in the emphasis given the drama's protagonist. At the same time, the grief and anguish of the mourners is, in effect, absorbed into the story of Colvin—an outsider, a Westerner—in a troubling way, similar to what I describe as a transfer of affect in *The Hurt Locker, Eye in the Sky,* and *Restrepo* (2010). The pathos the women enact marks a psychic and social space that is outside the ordinary Western frames for the performance of grief or sorrow. Yet the film continually returns to Colvin, in close-up, as if to translate the emotion of the historical flesh witnesses into the personal, psychological story of the main character.

Later that evening, while composing the story that would appear in the *Sunday Times* on May 18, 2003, Colvin loses the manuscript on her computer and, in a mild panic, appeals to her photographer Paul Conroy to recover it. Shortly after, she has a sexual encounter with another reporter that appears to be spontaneous and, in the context, somewhat surprising. The film wordlessly crosscuts their sex scene with images of traumatic ideation and memory. As the sounds of their lovemaking are heard on the soundtrack, the image track provides a grim montage of war deaths, injuries, and scenes of Colvin staggering drunkenly around her London flat, filtered through the subjective scrim of dream and memory. The sequence ends with her repeated words "Once you've seen, once you've seen." The film here

Marie Colvin reacting to the uncovering of the mass grave in Iraq. *A Private War,* directed by Mark Heineman, 2018. Produced by Matthew George, Mark Heineman, Basil Iwanyk, Marissa McMahon, and Charlize Theron.

Marie Colvin, photographer Paul Conroy, and Mourad, the Iraqi translator. *A Private War,* directed by Mark Heineman, 2018. Produced by Matthew George, Mark Heineman, Basil Iwanyk, Marissa McMahon, and Charlize Theron.

devises a radical ellipsis that transports Colvin from a hotel room in Iraq to her flat in London, which folds together images of death, injury, and sex in a montage that merges the objective and interior worlds in frightening scenes of traumatic ideation.

In joining these three moments—the recovery of the bodies in Iraq, the near loss of the story on her computer, and the montage of lovemaking and traumatic memory—the film channels Colvin's experience of discovering the mass grave into a reprise of traumatic scenes from her past, a return of repressed memory, laminating the experience of the disinterment with personal moments of visceral risk and shock. The montage brings the historical trauma of mass slaughter in Hussein's Iraq into the frame of private experience, a "private war," in which the public and the private, the external and the interior worlds, coalesce.

TWO MIRROR SCENES

Following the extended sequence in Iraq, her friend Rita (Nikki Amuka-Bird) convinces Colvin to seek treatment for PTSD. During the hospital sequence, her interior life is depicted in frightening detail, rendered as a kaleidoscope of images and sounds—memories of London parties overlaid by sounds of gunshots, images of Colvin running on hardscrabble hillsides, flashes of her wounding in Sri Lanka and her brutal treatment by the Sri Lankan soldiers. The cascade of mental images and sounds culminate with an image that we had seen earlier in a scene of psychic breakdown, a hallucinatory visual of a young girl, bleeding, lying on Colvin's bed. Following this montage scene, she has a long, probing conversation with her photographer, Conroy, who reveals that he too had once been hospitalized. Their discussion turns into a confession, as Colvin openly considers her compulsion to seek out the most risky and desperate conflict zones for her assignments. She tells Conroy that she is afraid of growing old, but that she doesn't want to die young; that she hates being in a war zone, "yet I feel compelled, compelled to see it for myself." Conroy, who earlier remarked that she has seen more war than most soldiers, tells her that that is because "she is addicted to it," a statement she does not contest.

Following her release from the hospital and the resumption of her frontline assignments—a return to the combat front that was suggested by her editor, Sean (Tom Hollander), on his visit to the hospital—Colvin shuttles among several combat hot spots, rendered in a series of vignettes that are juxtaposed with scenes in London. Here, a pattern develops: during the frontline conflict scenes summarized in this section, in Afghanistan, Palestine, and elsewhere, the film overlays several voice passages featuring Colvin's narration. Her measured, thoughtful prose reflections about war and the suffering of civilians, heard over hard-hitting images of death and injury in various locations, provides a kind of stabilizing frame. Surprisingly, a reflective mood takes hold in these scenes, as the spectator is provided with a capsule introduction to Colvin's "voice" as a journalist and a sense of the sweep of her combat experience. In London, however, the character's life is portrayed as increasingly fraught, with alcohol, unresolved trauma, and an encroaching awareness of mortality gnawing at her with growing insistence.

Toward the middle of the film, Colvin finds herself at a London party and introduces herself to the host, Tony Shaw (Stanley Tucci), with whom she has an immediate rapport. Their mutual attraction, the charming witticisms they exchange, mark this encounter as a potential way out of the cycle she has created, in which the adrenalin of combat reporting subsides into alcoholism and the afflictions of traumatic memory when she is not on assignment. The encounter with Shaw seems to have a tonic effect, as Colvin appears relaxed and happy the following morning—although Shaw tells her that she was shouting in her sleep. She is immediately drawn back into the crucible of war, however, as Libya has erupted in civil protest and the notorious Libyan leader Colonel Muammar Gaddafi has responded with mass violence against his own people. Colvin insists that she be assigned to cover this conflict.

The scenes set in Libya mark a turning point. Here, the extreme acts of violence Gaddafi enacts, which includes ordering the military to rape over one thousand Libyan girls as retribution for the popular uprising against him, bring Colvin face to face, in a direct way, with the leader of a monstrous regime that is making war on its own people. Moreover, she here confronts something new—the planned and deliberate targeting of journalists by the military. As shelling erupts outside the hotel where Colvin and other journalists are staying, she receives a text warning from her editor that the Libyans are targeting reporters so she is not to go to the front. As she is reading the message, a wounded man, hit by an explosive, is carried in on a stretcher. In a large room, several bodies have been placed on the floor, and several more are being attended to—journalists and photographers who have been shelled by Libyan soldiers in an RPG attack. Among the bloody bodies, she spots her friend, Norm (Corey Johnson), a conflict photographer. The camera dwells on the carnage in the room, and on Colvin's and Conroy's response to the killings. (The war photographer Tim Hetherington, whose work I consider in chapter 5, was also killed in an attack on journalists in Libya.)

Throughout the film, Colvin's ability to gain access to world leaders for exclusive interviews has been a kind of calling card, and true to form, she is invited to interview Gaddafi about his vicious response to his country's uprising. Gaddafi, whom Colvin has interviewed before, is one of the most unpredictable of the many despots Colvin has met, and the interview carries palpable risks.

Two scenes, shot in front of mirrors, frame the sequence of the interview with Gaddafi. In each, an iconography familiar from medieval and Renaissance painting is evoked—the imagery of beauty juxtaposed with portents of death. In the first mirror scene, Colvin is preparing for the upcoming interview, coughing, and lamenting Norm's death: "He was invincible!" As she stands in the bathroom, getting dressed, her photographer asks about her fancy bra. She responds, with some humor, that what she is wearing is not just a bra, it is the Italian luxury brand La Perla: "If anyone's going to pull my corpse from a trench, I want them to be impressed!" Immediately after this line, Colvin begins brushing her teeth. She starts to gag, reaches into her mouth, and pulls out a molar. The camera shifts to an over-the-shoulder shot, as she raises her eyes and regards herself in the mirror, a look that is held for a long moment.

Soon after the Gaddafi interview, characterized by barely concealed sexual threat throughout, we are presented with another mirror scene. Gaddafi has been captured and killed by the insurgents, and Colvin has published a prizewinning story about the horrors he has inflicted on the Libyan people and his ignoble end, "trapped in a sewer." She has just attended another gala awards ceremony, this time with Tony Shaw, who is now her partner, where she is again celebrated for her reporting. Immediately following the ceremony, we cut to Colvin in close-up, looking at herself in the mirror. She removes her eye patch, and for the first time we see the wounded eye, which she pries open. She then walks to a full-length mirror, regards herself naked, and turns to join Shaw in a candlelit bath.

The notion that war is truth—that it reveals the truth of the self and the world—is threaded through the film's treatment of Colvin's life and vocation. Explicitly articulated in the words she says during one of her breakdowns—"Once you've seen, once you've seen"—and in her emotional statement to her editor—"I see it so that you don't have to!"—the idea of war as negative revelation permeates the film's portrayal of both her masterful reporting as well as her episodes of trauma.[8] As the intimations of her own death become increasingly apparent, however, Colvin's insistence on the primacy of the act of "seeing it for myself" comes to seem like the working out of a pathological process. The loss of an eye, the loss of a tooth, the searching stares into the mirror signify not simply the embodied knowledge of war that Harari describes as flesh witnessing, but also a sense that her death is preordained, as if she has written a script for herself that she cannot alter. The eye patch, from this point in the film, does not reappear, as if the act of witnessing is now being ramped up to another level.

"I DON'T WANT MY WORDS TO BE INK ON PAPER"

The culminating scene of the film—the bombardment of Homs, Syria, by the Syrian military—stages Colvin's final act of reporting as a complex mixture of bearing witness to state terror being waged against its own people, and an act of sacrifice that verges on self-immolation. After a harrowing journey at night, with her driver dodging burning vehicles, gunshots, and explosions, Colvin and Conroy manage to get to the besieged neighborhood of Baba Amr. There, they are shown into a building where hundreds of civilians, mostly women and children, are huddled—a recall of the early scene in the tent camp in the forests of Sri Lanka. Here, Colvin interviews a young mother holding her baby in her arms; her breast milk has dried up, and she can feed her child only sugar and water. After hearing what they have suffered under the Syrian president Bashar al-Assad, who has been attacking his own citizens relentlessly, Colvin asks her, "Let me tell your story, I want people to know your story." The woman replies, "I don't want my words to be ink on paper. I want the world to know my story and that children are dying. A generation is dying . . . that's what I want the world to know."

In this statement, the film registers a historical shift. Testimony of war's suffering, from the young woman's viewpoint, is reduced by its representation in print, as if ink on paper could no longer effectively perform the function of bearing witness, of communicating the truth of war. The power of print journalism, the Syrian woman implies, has been superseded.

Colvin arranges to broadcast a story that will be run live, first on BBC Four, and then on CNN. Although her editor and her

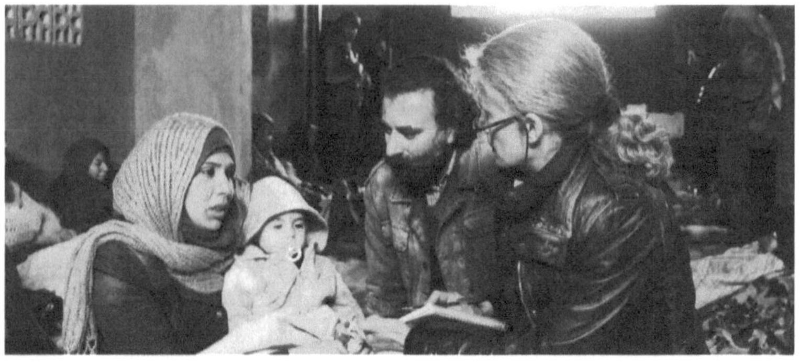

A Syrian woman interviewed by Marie Colvin: "I don't want my story to be words on paper." *A Private War,* directed by Mark Heineman, 2018. Produced by Matthew George, Mark Heineman, Basil Iwanyk, Marissa McMahon, and Charlize Theron.

photographer plead with her to leave the area, as plaster and debris is falling around her from nearby explosions, she insists on broadcasting, despite the risks. As the interview with CNN's Anderson Cooper unfolds, the camera focuses closely on Colvin, with occasional cutaways to her colleagues at the *Sunday Times* watching the coverage, to Tony Shaw, to her friend Rita. Speaking in a calm, collected voice, she explains that Homs has been shelled for eighteen straight days, that there are few rebels in the city, and that the Syrian government had lied when they repeatedly stated that they are only fighting against insurgents. The population being shelled consists not of rebels, except for a few scattered opposition militia members, but of twenty-eight thousand cold, starving civilians.

In the film, just prior to the broadcast, Colvin and Conroy had been depicted in a makeshift triage area, where the wounded are carried in to be treated by medical volunteers. As Conroy begins to film the scene, a child is brought in. Shrapnel has punctured the boy's chest; the man serving as a medic cannot save him. As the boy's father calls out to Allah, weeping and protesting, the camera cuts away to Conroy filming the scene, establishing a factual record, and placing Colvin in the room, at one point framed between the boy's mother and father. As rendered in *A Private War,* the footage here shot by Conroy is grafted into the broadcast interview.[9] Responding to Anderson Cooper's question about whether they should show images of a child dying, if it isn't "too much," Colvin says, "That little baby was one of two children who died today, one of children being injured every day. That baby probably will move more people to think, 'What is going on, and why is no one stopping this murder in Homs that is happening every day?'" Colvin's words, as presented in the film, are taken directly from the historical record of the CNN interview.

The broadcast on CNN confers a heightened level of authority on Colvin's reportage, bringing into a single frame the objectivity of journalistic voice, the veridical power of eyewitness presence on the scene, and the emotional conviction communicated by Conroy's video. Combining the gravitas of institutional journalism and the immediacy of unfiltered video images of suffering, the interview provides an emotionally potent mode of transmission, one that seems to proceed directly from the front lines into the distant lives of the viewers.

But the film has another agenda as well. Dramatic and powerful, the scene succeeds in transferring the affect, the pathos of suffering and victimization, from the civilian victims of Assad's murderous campaign to the character of Colvin herself, a tactic I have identified elsewhere in this film and in other films in this volume. As *A Private War* cuts to Colvin's editor, Sean, watching the interview in London with tears in his eyes, to her lover, Tony, listening silently, to her friend, Rita, viewing the interview with apprehension on her face, to Anderson Cooper as he lauds her courage for staying at the front—"one of the last Western reporters there"—the film shifts the emotion of wartime suffering away from the Syrian women and children under bombardment onto Colvin. Even the death of the child depicted in the broadcast seems to recede in importance. As we watch the other characters in the film listening to Colvin, as we see Conroy looking at her with concern as she reports the story—the pathos associated with the victims of war is transferred onto the Western protagonist.

THE TRUTH OF WAR

Colvin's death at the hands of the Syrian military almost immediately following the interview gives her final act of bearing witness depth and profundity, sealing its meaning and significance as a gesture of self-sacrifice. The film's dramatization of Colvin's life and death in war, the combination of genre patterns—war film and biopic—that shape the work around a moment of apotheosis in the final interview with CNN, now merge directly with historical events. The killing of Colvin and the French journalist Rémi Ochlik, along with the grave wounding of Conroy, by the Syrian government immediately predicates the reporter's statements about Assad and his attack on his own people. Her death becomes a form of testimony that reaches beyond her and Ochlik's demise, serving as unassailable proof of Assad's murderous campaign.[10]

The film ends with a return to its opening shot. With the camera again situated overhead, peering down at the rubble of the building that had sheltered Colvin and the other journalists in Homs, her voice returns to its opening narration, repeating her response concerning how fear comes afterward, "when it's all over." Only her legs are visible in the shot; the upper half of her body is obscured under brick and concrete. The camera slowly zooms back to provide a view of the bombed-out city of Homs, its ruins extending from horizon to horizon.

The explicitly circular structure of the film, with Colvin's death in Homs both initiating and concluding the narrative, suggests an alpha and omega construction, the end inscribed at the beginning—a circular structure that appears in a number of war films. The formal repetition that marks the beginnings and the endings of films—such as *All Quiet on the Western Front* (1930), *Apocalypse Now* (1979), *Saving Private Ryan*, *Letters from Iwo Jima* (2006), and *The Hurt Locker*, among many others—might be read mainly as a poetic reiteration, a reprise of the themes and motifs that pattern the film. Elisabeth Bronfen, however, argues that the recursive structure of the war film serves to reframe the work, shifting the focus to larger questions of history and memory. She begins her excellent study of American war cinema with a powerful analysis of the final shot of *All Quiet on the Western Front*: "On screen, death can be reversed, the young men who have died in the trenches of World War I resurrected. . . . The young men on the screen are revenants, actors playing undead soldiers who will not stay in their graves."[11]

In *A Private War*, the repetition of the opening aerial shot, accompanied by Colvin's disembodied voice, merges the spectral theme of war as an endless cycle of violence, of "walking forever into battle," as Bronfen has it, with the theme of remembrance, of the survivor who remains to tell the story. In this case, Colvin herself appears to be constructed as the narrator of her own story, as if she were looking back in time, from the moment of her death. Colvin's opening and closing dialogue about writing her own obituary gives her voice and words particular force, as we hear her speaking over the image of her own dead body half buried in rubble. Then, as the camera tilts to reveal the ruins of Homs, the film cuts to a shot of the actual Marie Colvin, looking into the camera and speaking the lines we have been listening to, as if she were directly addressing the viewer—an uncanny juxtaposition of life and death, fiction and reality. The two voices, Colvin's and the voice of the actor playing her (Rosamund Pike), sound identical. The film then closes with a montage of newspaper headlines and stories, starting with the dispatches from Homs, then going back in time, to the stories from Libya and Iraq, and back to 1988 when Colvin first began reporting on war.

If what I take as the film's larger project—its exposure of the murder of civilians as an increasingly frequent tactic of war—remains a challenge to representation, it is perhaps because of these acts' "unspeakable history." As Guynn points out, the filmmakers of works such as *The Act of Killing* (dir. Joshua Oppenheimer, 2012), *S-21: The Khmer Rouge Killing Machine* (dir. Rithy Panh, 2003), and *Nostalgia for the Light* (dir. Patricio Guzmán, 2010), all of which deal with atrocities against civilians by their own governments, found existing genre forms to be incapable of registering the scale and the significance of this form of violence in modern historical life. Each filmmaker found it necessary to create a new formal and symbolic language to depict content that was seen to be almost unrepresentable.

A Private War takes a different approach, rendering the violence of war and the suffering of its victims through the filter of individual witnessing, commentary, and trauma, dilating it to serve as a reflection of the world and of war in its current state. This complex symbolic solution to what is clearly not simply a formal problem has both strengths and weaknesses. On the one hand, it allows the film to engage with the reality of contemporary world conflict, in a range of disparate locations, by situating the suffering and chaos of lives lost and shattered in the experience and psychology of a compelling Western protagonist. On the other, the individualistic focus of the biopic complicates any attempt to render collective, historical experience, as the suffering of the civilian victims of numerous murderous regimes is registered mainly through its impact on the emotional life of the conflict journalist.

As the protagonist of a war narrative with none of the standard war film themes, filmed in a variety of conflict locations, Colvin's story reframes the experience of violence in war explicitly around the act of bearing witness. In some ways, she stands as an exemplar of the changing character of modern war—her words, far from serving simply as reportage, are taken as the equivalent of weapons of war. The struggle over control of the narrative, the aggressive attempts by state actors—governments, soldiers, and police—to suppress critical and competing narratives of events, is shown to be as important as the struggle on the ground. And as journalists continue to be assassinated, imprisoned, dismembered, spied on, and harassed for exposing the lies of the agents of contemporary violence, the story of Marie Colvin can be taken as a paradigm of the ways that both distant and nearby wars entangle the whole of the social and historical order.

In other ways, however, Colvin stands outside of any paradigm. She has "seen more war than most soldiers," as Conroy says; nonetheless she rejects the suggestion that she has PTSD, because "that's what soldiers get," not journalists. She places herself repeatedly on the front lines, bringing into close observation the tragic victims of war; but she also seeks out interviews with strongmen and dictators, including Muammar Gaddafi. Her determination to see for herself the suffering of the innocent victims of war, ceaselessly entering and reentering the hellish landscapes of contemporary war, comes to seem like a release, a palliative for her even more torturous interior life, as traumatic memory and hallucination run rampant when she is home in London and not under external threat.

The range of topics explored in *A Private War*—the psychological damage caused by exposure to war, the murderous military campaigns by governments against civilians, the targeting of journalists, and the courage of conflict journalists in bringing to light atrocities that would otherwise go unrecorded—are all expressed in the story of a single historical figure. That the figure is a woman should come as no surprise, given the real-world transformations as well as the transformations of the war film genre this book has described. Nevertheless, *A Private War* stands as a particularly strong example of the changing narratives of war in contemporary cinema, and the emergence of women characters as the subjects and the agents of the drama.

CHAPTER 5

FOUR ELEGIES OF WAR

Restrepo, Infidel, Into the Korengal, and Sleeping Soldiers—single screen

THE DOCUMENTARY FILMS AND PHOTOGRAPHS made by Tim Hetherington and Sebastian Junger in the Korengal Valley in Afghanistan raise several troubling questions of war representation, which are both specific to documentary film practice in the contemporary period of U.S. war and more broadly connected to the history of genre. Produced almost entirely under the constraints of embedment—the filmmakers were ensconced with a U.S. infantry company in Afghanistan for over a year—the multiple works they produced provide a largely sympathetic and personal portrait of the soldiers of Battle Company, reflecting the intimate acquaintance the filmmakers developed with the men, as well as their dependence on them for protection in an active combat zone. The formal design of some parts of this work, however—in particular, the shaping of documentary images into an elegy defined by emotional reminiscence—gives rise to questions that go beyond the limitations imposed by embedment, touching on fundamental codes of the war film genre and its dependence on the cultivation of pathos as a principal mode of rhetorical address.

The war in Afghanistan has so far received minimal representation in film, with few documentaries and even fewer dramatic fiction films taking the Afghan war as their subject. Its near invisibility in American culture gives the full-length film *Restrepo* (2010), the photo series *Infidel* (2010) and *Into the Korengal* (2011), as well as the short video *Sleeping Soldiers—single screen* (2009) an almost unique status, providing firsthand observations of an unfamiliar environment—an embattled army outpost in what was one of the most remote and contested regions of the world. The four projects bring into relief different aspects of contemporary war, highlighted by nuances of representation and historical reference that the various media employed in these projects allow.

The works I treat here bring into sharp focus many of the critical questions I have foregrounded in this book, including the performance of gender, the residual presence of the rescue narrative, and the imagery of pathos as a fundamental code of the cinema of war. The project also illuminates the importance of genre memory, both in the shaping of the narrative and in its pictorial compositions. Where these films and photographs stand apart from the other works I consider in this study, however, is in the pointed questions they elicit concerning objectivity, cooperation, and the possibility of critical voice in the exceptional circumstances of embedment. One writer has faulted *Restrepo* for seeming to be complicit with the acts of the soldiers, calling it a "paramilitary film."[1] Another writer has underscored the filmmakers' recycling of familiar visual tropes of the traumatized soldier, especially in an award-winning photograph included in the photo collection produced by Hetherington and Junger titled *Infidel*.[2] The short video-essay *Sleeping Soldiers—single screen*, composed of footage taken during the deployment, has also been criticized for its lack of critical perspective. Although *Sleeping Soldiers* is innovative and powerful, Erina Duganne writes, it is symptomatic of the general willingness of journalists and the viewing public to accept, unchallenged, the practice of embedment, the restrictions that go along with it, and the almost inevitable sense of identification with the soldiers that ensues.[3] On the other side of the critical divide, Saumava Mitra has discussed a short photo-essay by Hetherington titled *Into the Korengal* (2011). Mitra argues that Hetherington has woven a "counter-hegemonic" discourse into images of conflict, particularly in his exploration of Afghan masculinity; photos in the essay range from the elders of the Korengal to young male children, offering a striking contrast with the styles of masculinity that characterize the young U.S. soldiers represented in *Restrepo* and *Infidel*.[4]

In this chapter, I focus on the work of Hetherington and Junger in the Korengal Valley as examples of war representation conditioned by the constraints and potentials of embedment, poised between cooperation and critical voice. The genre memory encoded in the visual language of war cinema and photography provides a set of resources for a complex reading of these works. As I have argued elsewhere, genres remember the past and make their resources available for the present. When an older genre is adapted for new uses, in a new context, it produces a double voicing. In the work of Hetherington and Junger, I argue, the genre of the war film is invested with a secondary accent, a double voicing that in certain scenes and images suggests an alternative, or "counter-hegemonic," point of view woven into the body of their work.[5]

I begin with the centerpiece of the overall project, the feature-length film *Restrepo*. Shot during a combat operation that extended over the period 2007–9 and its immediate aftermath, the film juxtaposes two distinct cinematic vocabularies. Footage from the filmmakers' twelve-month embedment with Battle Company in Outpost Restrepo, depicting life in the outpost and the battles as they occurred, is counterpointed with individual interviews filmed in Italy immediately after the soldiers' active-duty assignments were complete. The title of the film designates both the setting for the deployment—OP Restrepo—and the memorial arc of the documentary, as the outpost was named for Private Juan Sebastián "Doc" Restrepo, a medic who was killed early in the deployment.

The twelve-month duration of the filmmakers' embedment and the range of events depicted—which include a tribal elders' wary meeting with the U.S. commanding officer, patrols in nearby villages, a fatal mission called Rock Avalanche, and the close observation of daily life in the outpost—lends the film a sense of vérité authenticity. The marines are portrayed in summer and winter, playing guitar, showing off their tattoos, defending the outpost, patrolling the surrounding countryside, and attempting to fight the Taliban in the steep mountain terrain. The film arouses a sense of deep wariness, however, with its mute observation of soldiers targeting and shooting a man on the mountain paths, who may or may not have been an enemy fighter, and its hasty panning away from the covered body of a tribal Afghan killed in a U.S. raid.

In contrast to the largely observational tone of these sequences, a powerful sense of pathos dominates the post-deployment interviews with soldiers from OP Restrepo. Alone on camera, bathed in studio lighting, the soldiers relate experiences of trauma, loss, and continued suffering; they are unable to sleep, troubled by memories and nightmares, and unwilling to forget the comrades they have lost. The film plays out in a dualistic fashion, partly a celebration of what Kristin Whissel calls the masculine "rhetoric of soldiery," and partly an emotional lament for the dead.[6]

In considering these questions, I am interested, first, in exploring whether certain details of visual design in the film *Restrepo* can be read as a form of narrative commentary, perhaps giving the work a more critical accent than some of the writers above have discerned. Elements of mise-en-scène, the way certain shots are extended beyond a conventional or necessary duration, the counterpoint of voice and image, at times suggest points of tension between the military perspective and the filmmakers' viewpoint. While explicit criticism or obvious counterargument would clearly fall outside the limits imposed by embedment, close analysis of certain scenes brings into view an undercurrent, a distancing perspective that is both nuanced and, to my mind, effective. In certain sequences, the history of war cinema is evoked in a way that expands the potential meaning of the action being recorded. Hetherington has made this point explicitly: "We all carry an image library in our heads, that we can cross-reference to create layers of meaning."[7]

Three sequences from *Restrepo* illustrate the complexity of its narrative address: the council with the tribal elders, in which Captain Dan Kearney, the commanding officer, attempts to convince the elders to lend intelligence and help to the American military; the follow-up military patrol after the bombardment of a small mountain village, which may or may not have been harboring Taliban fighters; and the scene called Rock Avalanche, in which one soldier from Battle Company is killed.

The loya jirga, the meeting of the council of elders with representatives of Battle Company, occurs early in the film. Kearney eagerly tries to convey the benefits of cooperating with the Americans on the building of a road. As the elders sit in a circle on the floor, with Kearney seated among them, he begins by promising jobs, money, and access to health care in exchange for their support. The elders appear to have come straight out of the Old Testament, with long, hennaed beards, turbans, and robes. Early in the discussion, the camera isolates one elder attempting to pierce a juice packet with a small straw. Turning the packet over and over in his hands, trying different angles of attack, he is unable to push the straw through to access the refreshment the American military has handed out to the council. As Kearney continues to speak, at length, about the advantages of cooperating with the American military, the film lingers in close-up on the man's attempt to master this commonplace product from the Western world. Here, the gulf between the two orders of civilization, two modes of production, is brought home: the close-up rendering of the struggle with the juice pack can be read as a wordless commentary, a reframing of Kearney's all too familiar rhetoric of U.S. beneficence: a synecdoche for the American mission as a whole, ill-considered and unworkable. More broadly, the sequence might be understood as a comment on U.S.–Afghan strategy at the time, based on what General David Petraeus called counterterrorism—the attempt to cultivate relationships of influence and dependency among the local population. The scene underscores the infantilizing approach of the U.S. government toward the tribal population, condensed in a product associated with Western children.

A different critical argument can be drawn from another major scene, the follow-up to a large-scale U.S. helicopter attack on a mountain village. Here, genre memory plays a role, as the sequence centers, in its camera work and editing, on children wounded in the bombardment. As several soldiers from Battle Company move through the village after the attack, they discover that the assault has killed five tribal Afghans and wounded several women and children. It is unclear whether there were Taliban in the village, as the soldiers are unable to recover any direct evidence. Instead, the camera observes the wreckage of a mountain home, a demolished kitchen, a woman quietly lying on a bed surrounded by her children, and then notices—and quickly pans away from—the covered body of an Afghan man. The film focuses at length, however, on a crying infant and two little girls, one with serious injuries, her eyes bloodied and swollen, and another with dried blood on her face. The crying infant, held closely by an Afghan man, is spattered with blood.

The resonance of genre memory is evoked in this scene, bringing

A wounded Afghan child after a U.S. raid. *Restrepo*, directed by Tim Hetherington and Sebastian Junger, 2010. Produced by Tim Hetherington, Sebastian Junger, and Nick Quested.

into view the full symbolic power of the image of the child in war, a silent commentary utilizing one of the oldest of cinematic tropes. An icon of the malevolence of war, the image of the wounded or dead child is woven into the history of the genre, visible in classic works such as *Battleship Potemkin* (1925), *Germany Year Zero* (1948), and *Apocalypse Now* (1979), and serving an especially important role in the contemporary films I treat in this volume, *The Hurt Locker* (2008), *Eye in the Sky* (2015), and *A Private War* (2018). In this scene, *Restrepo* summons this pictorial and narrative tradition, producing charged affective signals in its close-ups of wounded children. The indelible photograph of the young Vietnamese girl fleeing from a U.S. napalm attack is not far from the viewer's mind either, an association underlined by multiple shots of U.S. helicopters attacking the mountain village in the preceding scene.

The image of the wounded child typically communicates an unambiguous anti-war sentiment, providing a distilled moment of concentrated emotion that stands apart from the rest of the film. In the scene at the village, the shots of wounded children create a point of rupture, a suspension of focalizing perspective with the soldiers of Battle Company. Explicitly evoking a long-established visual discourse of lament and empathy for the innocent victims of war, the scene creates a powerful current of affect, which might be interpreted as the filmmakers' dissent from the military campaign in Afghanistan.

As the film unfolds, however, the image of the child in war comes to accent the portrayals of the young U.S. soldiers themselves. Several of the soldiers are teenagers, seen in moments of high tension and vulnerability, both in live-action sequences and in the post-deployment interviews that are interspersed throughout the film. Quietly mourning the loss of their comrades, one soldier openly weeping, the soldiers of Battle Company appear in these scenes to have little of the bravado or attitude that fiction films often associate with young men in war, a type of masculine performance that filters into even recent works such as *The Hurt Locker, Fury* (2014), *Lone Survivor* (2013), and *Generation Kill* (2008).

The vulnerability of the soldiers, which comes to form a secondary theme of the film, emerges fully with the death of Sergeant Larry Rougle. Occurring near the end of the work, the incident draws into a single frame the adrenalized action of combat and the pathos of the young soldier first witnessing violent death. As the company attempts to assert control over an area controlled by the Taliban, the operation, named Rock Avalanche, comes to be fraught with difficulty. The steep terrain and the soldiers' murky understanding of the Taliban fighters' positions leads to dangerous scattering and isolation, with soldiers strung out in the forest in groups of two and three. Sergeant Rougle, one of the best soldiers in Battle Company, has somehow been separated and killed. The camera discovers the body of Rougle at about the same time the nearby soldiers do. The filmmakers maintain a discreet distance from his corpse, keeping his face out of frame, concentrating instead on the reactions of the individual soldiers as they come into view and learn of his death. One man, told by the sergeant in charge that it is Rougle, cannot contain himself, breaking into open weeping, his voice high-pitched and anxious as he repeatedly exclaims that it can't be Rougle. Another soldier must be quietly assured, several times, that the sergeant died instantly. The film provides close-ups on certain details, fixing on the dead man's boots, on the blood-soaked back and pants of another soldier, on the bloodied hands of a man aiming a weapon.

The manner in which the fallen soldier is rendered in films of war often provides an index of the film's larger themes. In classic films such as *All Quiet on the Western Front* (1930) and *Saving Private Ryan* (1998), the constellation of meanings surrounding the fallen comrade touches on the way the two different wars—World War I and World War II—were perceived in the historical period in which the works were made. In *All Quiet on the Western Front,* for example, death is so commonplace, as Stanislaus Katczinsky (Kat, played by Louis Wolheim), the grizzled mentor to the young soldiers explains, that the corpse of their fallen comrade must be ignored. In the words of Kat, "It's a corpse, that's all it is. I don't care if it's your friend, leave it there." Apart from the protracted scene between Paul Bäumer (Lew Ayres), the lead character, and the French soldier he has killed, there is little overt emotion expressed in the film toward the dead—no ritual of mourning, no solemn graveyard scenes. Even the death of Kat at the end of the film seems to be barely registered by Paul. In *All Quiet on the Western Front,* death in war is without meaning, a sad and grotesque waste.

By contrast, in *Saving Private Ryan,* the death of the medic, Technician Fourth Grade Irwin Wade, is rendered in an extended scene saturated with emotion. His death serves as a catalyst for the company of soldiers. On the verge of mutiny in the immediate aftermath of Wade's killing, the leader of the company, Captain John Miller, confesses his doubts, and also speaks of his need to earn his way back home, a speech that embodies the ideals of the World War II citizen-soldier. Wade's death and the mourning crystallized in Miller's words consolidate the company's resolve; at his gravesite, they renew their commitment to the search for Ryan. The rescue scenario that provides the dominant narrative pattern of the American war film in the late twentieth-century emerges fully here, bathing the scene in the symbolism of reparation and redemption.[8] And as the sequence concludes, the camera consecrates the moment, capturing the light at sunset and framing the battlefield, with its barbed wire and craters, in an extended low-angle shot, with a fully foliated tree in the background, spreading its branches over the field as Miller is silhouetted on a ridge. In *Saving Private Ryan,* death in battle takes on sacrificial value; the death of the soldier is meaningful. The fallen soldier will be remembered.

The death of Rougle falls somewhere between these two poles. The soldiers of Battle Company respond with strong emotion on

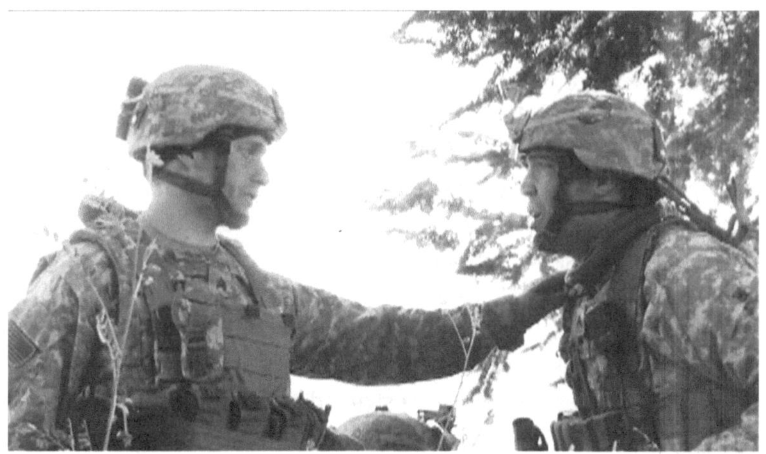

A soldier reacting to the death of Sergeant Rougle. *Restrepo,* directed by Tim Hetherington and Sebastian Junger, 2010. Produced by Tim Hetherington, Sebastian Junger, and Nick Quested.

the battlefield; shock, dismay, and disbelief seem to stagger the men when they first see his body. In the interviews following his death, moreover, the memory of his loss surfaces repeatedly. The death of the soldier, however, is not mapped into any kind of consoling metanarrative in the film; unlike *Saving Private Ryan,* the larger themes of sacrifice and redemption are not available in *Restrepo,* nor is the antiwar condemnation of war's waste that overarches the many deaths portrayed in *All Quiet on the Western Front.* The pathos of death is expressed only in the painful internal reflections of the individual members of Battle Company. As in *The Hurt Locker,* with only the solitary mourner, Sergeant J. T. Sanborn, paying muted respect to his team leader's effects, the death of Rougle is without any larger, collective meaning.

During the post-deployment interviews, the soldiers, filmed in what is at times extreme close-up on a darkened set, are frequently overcome by emotion, sometimes breaking into tears. In a recent study comparing soldier memoires from the World War I period with military blogs and memoires of the present day, Lilie Chouliaraki describes the mode of address and self-presentation of contemporary soldier memoires as emotionalized, characterized by testimony that is overtly intimate and responsive to loss. The open disclosure of the soldier's psychological vulnerability, a constant in these memoires, stands in sharp contrast to the conventions of World War I memoirists, where irony, a flattening of emotion, and a displacement of affect into tones of disillusionment and fatalism are emblematic. Irony, in the period following World War I, came to define the age, "a virtual allegory of the political and social cognition of our time."[9] In contrast, the "war on terror" memoires, Chouliaraki writes, are defined by a confessional mode of address that, she surmises, may be connected to the media discourses of contemporary war and what she says is its ubiquity and prominence in contemporary representation: "Private feelings, including soldiers' war-related traumas and PTSD pathologies, cease to be restricted to the domestic sphere and have become visible." The soldier is now positioned as a witness who shares his experience with others and "invites those others to give a moral response to his testimonies of loss and suffering."[10]

Although I find much to agree with in Chouliaraki's perceptive essay, I feel that the interviews in *Restrepo* serve a different role, focused, as they are, on the larger themes of loss, trauma, and the isolation of the individual soldiers who are now separated from their troop. The film, in my view, raises an immanent critique of U.S. war culture in the current period, especially the social and institutional indifference to the costs and sacrifices of war—despite the widespread appropriation of the imagery, weapons, and uniforms of the military in popular culture.

Closely attuned to the long history of war cinema, *Restrepo* attempts to situate its documentary portrayal of the soldiers of Battle Company in what appears, at first glance, to be a new iteration of a genre tradition. Focusing closely on behavioral detail, the work portrays the camaraderie of the outpost, the deadly firefights, and the poignancy of loss as a contemporary take on what are now familiar scenes. The frames of genre memory, however, also bring into view the stark differences between the film's depiction of modern war and the stories and images of the past. For example, a good deal of the film exemplifies what Sebastian Junger describes as the "truth of combat as a form of bonding," that war is the "only chance men have to love each other unconditionally."[11] Several sequences depict soldiers wrestling, comparing tattoos, working out together, and in one scene dancing, in a close group, to the Günther and the Sunshine Girls' 2004 Europop hit "Touch Me." Undercutting the tone of warm familiarity and physical, communal affection, however, are scenes of psychological distress, both in the interviews and in live-action scenes, in which the men are isolated and clearly at the edge. *Restrepo* employs frequent hard cuts from soldiers in intimate close-up, in anxious recollection, directly to live action in the combat zone, as if the film were hurling the soldiers headlong from introspection into a firefight. The radical shifts in tone create a dualism in the narrative rhetoric that is difficult to frame in terms of affect, giving the work a disturbing, unsettled feeling.

INFIDEL: TWO PHOTOGRAPHS

These themes are also illustrated in the book of photographs, *Infidel*, taken during the same period of embedment as *Restrepo*. Performative masculinity and its opposite—the loneliness, isolation, and trauma of combat experience—both come into high relief in two exemplary images, a picture Hetherington called "Man Eden," and a photo of a lone soldier, Specialist Brandon Olson, in the immediate aftermath of battle (the latter of which won the 2008 World Press Photo Award). Although many of the photographs in *Infidel* show the soldiers performing the "rhetoric of soldiery," in Whissel's evocative phrase—shots in which men are fighting, posing with weapons and ammunition, or working out—"Man Eden" stands apart. A large, two-page photograph, it is placed at the exact center of the book. In this work, a small group of shirtless soldiers from OP Restrepo are pictured shoveling dirt into bags that will be used to reinforce their bunker. The golden lighting, the muscled torsos, the poses of relaxation and exertion, all communicate a sense of nonchalant grace and physical pleasure in work. Task performance, the camaraderie of life in the open—"Man Eden" recalls the well-known trope of ordinary life in the military camp, first seen in the Spanish–American War films of Thomas Edison's 1898–99 series, and later, among many other representations, in Edward Steichen's portrayals of navy servicemen in World War II.[12] An impression of harmony is evoked in this image, crosshatched in a complex way by our awareness of what lies just outside the frame: the gun emplacements, the barbed wire, the Taliban fighters. Removed momentarily from the terror and mortal risk that surrounds them, the soldiers communicate the potential of youth; the pathological side of combat—its tearing of bodies and minds—is here bracketed from the frame. War enters the image only obliquely, in the physical togetherness of the men in the outpost, and in the echoes of other, earlier wars that reverberate in the viewer's mind.

In the second photo, an image of the exhausted, possibly traumatized soldier Brandon Olson, Hetherington captures a young man in full combat gear a few moments after he has left the battle zone. Leaning back, his hand to his face, the soldier radiates distress. The blurriness of the photograph reinforces the sense of traumatic aftershock. Wide-eyed, looking vaguely toward the camera, the subject seems only partially aware of the photographer: the photo asks us to imagine what he has just witnessed, to see into the world expressed in the image, to see through the soldier's eyes at events that have just occurred. The fraternal imagery of the earlier photo, "Man Eden," has disappeared. What remains is a vision of isolation, a suggestion of psychological injury, and a gesture—one hand held to his face, the other covering one eye—that signals an effort to blot from view the events he has just witnessed, while at the same time remembering them with dread. This is the closing photograph in *Infidel*.

The only photo of its kind in the collection, the image evokes an extensive figural history: Don McCullin's portrait of a traumatized soldier in Vietnam (1968), Larry Burrough's photo of a wounded marine (1966), Pablo Picasso's *Guernica* (1937), and Francisco Goya's *Disasters of War* (1810–20) are not far from view. With this image of battlefield trauma, Hetherington brings the war in Afghanistan into dialogue with a different pictorial tradition of war than that of "Man Eden," foregrounding the immediate corporeal reality of combat and connecting to a photographic history of injury and violence, both emotional and physical. As the press release for the World Press Photo Award affirms, "This image represents the exhaustion of a man—and the exhaustion of a nation. . . . We're all connected to this. It's a picture of a man at the end of a line."

The photo of Olson has elicited several different critical responses, many taking issue with what I see as a strength—its invocation of genre memory. Two of the award jurors in 2008, for example, called Hetherington's image "a predictable World Press Photo Award winner, an amalgam of all the images of war and death that we have embedded in our memory." The visual trope of the worn-out soldier, they write, "cast[s] the world in the same mold over and over again."[13] Images of the Afghan conflict, as another writer says, "have remained remarkably similar in both content and approach. US forces are the locus of the narrative and combat scenes are repeatedly pictured . . . in a way that foregrounds competing American military interests."[14]

When paired with "Man Eden," however, the Olson photograph communicates a somewhat different message, highlighting the changing meanings associated with war in the twenty-first century. In these two images, the contrast between a community of enlisted men and the isolation and psychological pain of the solitary soldier comes to the fore. In a recent essay, Junger argues that the increase in cases of PTSD, which is now epidemic despite the small number of soldiers engaged in active combat, is due in large part to the soldiers' withdrawal from an idea of community, their removal from the collective experience that defined the battle zone. The sense of shared risk and exposure manifest in combat is erased when soldiers return from war, where isolation, incomprehension, and social indifference are the dominant experiences. Junger concludes that the critical sense of a "shared public meaning" for war is entirely missing in American culture.[15] In the juxtaposition of these two photographs, the pain and loss of war is also projected forward in time, suggesting the experience of isolation that awaits the returning soldier. The title Hetherington gave the first image, "Man Eden," also communicates this theme, albeit obliquely, as an Eden is always a lost Eden, a place to which one cannot return.

INTO THE KORENGAL

The short photo-essay by Hetherington *Into the Korengal*, published in 2011, departs from the almost exclusive focus on American troops that typically defines the work of embedded photographers and journalists in Afghanistan; instead, it centers on Afghan males, of different ages, interacting with the soldiers of Battle Company. The photo-essay, though short—it contains only eight images, accompanied by Hetherington's written commentary—is instructive. The photography scholar Saumava Mitra argues that these images suggest an incipient counternarrative to the one-sided depictions in Western media, showing Afghan men engaging with and reacting to U.S. soldiers in a way that reveals something of the emotional dynamics of occupation. In the first photo, an Afghan elder is seen negotiating with the commanding officer of OP Restrepo, asserting the innocence of a fellow tribesman held prisoner and attempting to bargain his release in exchange for the villagers' cooperation. In another, a different elder is pictured holding a baby injured by a U.S. bombing strike, as if he were presenting evidence to the American soldiers of the results of their mission. In another photo, a young boy, also injured during the airstrike, regards the soldiers with explicit anger and fear. A young Afghan man, in a different photo, glowers at a U.S. soldier who is fingerprinting him. Finally, the closing image depicts a dozen or more young boys, gathered together and sitting on the ground outside a school, with a large grenade launcher pictured in the foreground.

Mitra observes that the arrangement of the images portray the males of the Korengal in reverse chronology, moving from photos of elders, to working-age men, to young boys, as if to imply that the U.S. military occupation has affected multiple generations, and suggesting that the impact of the occupation on the tribal peoples of the region will continue for a long time. Tellingly, the few U.S. soldiers depicted in these images appear indifferent to the gazes of the Afghan males. The Afghans' expressions of anger, fear, appeals for understanding, or a wary avoidance are simply not noticed, as if they were irrelevant. In the fingerprinting shot, for example, two U.S. soldiers stand in the outpost, towering over an Afghan man who looks at them with resentment. Both U.S. soldiers are shirtless; one is heavily tattooed and the other is shadowed by the plastic netting overhead. They exhibit an almost smug sense of dominance and control.

Images from "outside the wire," as Mitra calls them, are unusual: in the Hetherington archive that is now housed in the British Imperial War Museum, only 35 of the 374 photos he made in the Korengal feature Afghan boys or men. Images of Afghan males are similarly rare in the film *Restrepo*. Nonetheless, where they appear, they are effective, working as counterpoint to the subjective Western image library concerning Afghanistan masculinity, usually conceived as "belligerent, dead, or absent," in Mitra's words.[16]

SLEEPING SOLDIERS—SINGLE SCREEN

Sleeping Soldiers—single screen provides a different kind of counterpoint, depicting the soldiers of Battle Company asleep in their bunks. A video-essay made from images and acoustic material excerpted from the footage for *Restrepo*, the soldiers of Battle Company appear inordinately young, with none of the posturing or masculine iconography to which we have become accustomed. Hetherington remarked that "you never see them like this," that "they always look so tough . . . but when they're asleep they look like little boys. They look the way their mothers probably remember them. . . . You can see their youth and vulnerability."[17] Superimposed over their faces, however, are scenes of war and the sounds of battle—multiple layers of image and sound are blended over different shots, as one sleeping soldier gives way to another. Although the topic of sleeping soldiers is a traditional subject of photography, painting, and printmaking, dating to at least the 1630s, the video-essay by Hetherington expands the frame of representation in a distinctive way, capturing an inner world dominated by memories of threat, insecurity, and blood. The voices of soldiers in distress, the sounds of gunfire close by, the near panic caused by combat gone wrong—the haunted dream life of the soldiers is rendered as fragments of remembered experience that return to lay claim to the present.

With its extended closeups, stylized acoustics, and dilation of certain details, the video creates an eerie, associative rhetoric of war images. Shots of blood spattered on a military uniform are followed by an extreme close-up of blood caked on a soldier's hand as he grips his rifle. The soft faces of Afghan children loom into view, to be replaced by the gaunt, bearded visage of an Afghan elder speaking in dialect and gesticulating. In some shots, large, cumulus clouds seem to drift over the faces of the soldiers, followed by shots of airborne helicopters as seen from the ground.

The through line of the video-essay emerges in its second half. The death of Sergeant Rougle on the mountain, an incident that also forms the nexus of the film *Restrepo*, coalesces as the dominant narrative event of *Sleeping Soldiers*. In the short video, the discovery of Rougle's body unfolds in a more realistic idiom than the drifting superimpositions seen earlier; the oneiric mix of layered images and echoing sounds from the first half of the video subside. Now, themes of conscience and guilt come into relief. As the soldiers huddle in the bush around the body of Rougle, the stylized audio track combines sounds of a soldier weeping, the quiet reassurances of the commanding officer, an odd, electronic beeping signal, and other acoustic traces that are panned across the auditory landscape. The video closes with a return to an image of a soldier asleep, supine, stretched out on a top bunk, a pose distinct from that of the other soldiers portrayed in the video. Here, no dream images are superimposed, only the sound of a soldier's soft, off-screen voice saying "It's not your fault." In its three-minute duration, the video captures the penetration of war's violence into the inner fabric of psychic life.

Hetherington's *Sleeping Soldiers—single screen,* like its counterparts *Restrepo* and *Infidel,* has provoked questions about the possibilities for critique within the overall politics of embedment. Duganne commends the video for documenting the brutalities of war and reflecting on its emotional complexities. She maintains, however, that the close, intimate gaze that the practice of embedding allows necessarily works against the critical potential of visual representations of war: "In the end the installation does nothing to disrupt the combined effects that these representations of conflict have had on our visual understanding of the war in Afghanistan, including most importantly, the collusion of the US military with them. . . . *Sleeping Soldiers* is the product of an embedding system that has likewise gone unchecked by the mainstream press."[18]

Duganne's points are important, touching on the major issue of identification and complicity on the part of photographers and journalists with the military establishment. Indeed, little of the body of work Hetherington and Junger produced in Afghanistan could be said to "disrupt" our visual understanding of recent U.S. wars. However, I read the video *Sleeping Soldiers* somewhat differently than does Duganne. As in my earlier discussions of *Restrepo* and the photographs in *Infidel,* I argue that a critical voice, a dissenting viewpoint, can be found in details of framing, duration, and emphasis, and in the work's appeal to genre memory. Although *Sleeping Soldiers—single screen* necessarily foregrounds the perspective of the soldiers of Battle Company, as Duganne suggests, another set of messages emerges from its focus on the aftereffects of violence, bringing to the surface a vein of resistance to what I will call the social ethos that surrounds contemporary war. In particular, the video raises important questions concerning the place of traumatic memory in the narrative of twenty-first-century war, and the role of psychic and moral injury in the symbolic codex that has begun to take shape around the soldiers of these wars. Foregrounding themes of guilt, troubled memory, trauma, and the pathos of loss, the dreamwork imagery of the video-essay takes on a public task. With its wide visibility on YouTube and Vimeo, *Sleeping Soldiers—single screen* might be read as a minor-key, moving image memorial, a place keeper for the missing memorials to the soldiers suffering from psychic injury—a kind of anti-memorial, opening a space of reflection rather than imposing a clarified meaning.

Drawing on the genre memory of over a century of war cinema, *Restrepo, Infidel, Into the Korengal,* and *Sleeping Soldiers—single screen* cast a new light on some of the oldest conventions of the form: the fraternal community of soldiers; the symbolic conversion of meaningless death into meaningful sacrifice; the suffering and cruelty of war condensed in the figure of the wounded or dead child. Each of these themes, however, are countered by their opposite. The fraternal community of affection is set against the isolation of postdeployment. The culture of remembrance attached to the death of one soldier, Doc Restrepo, for whom the film and the outpost is named, is countered by the bitter, uncelebrated death of Sergeant Rougle. The pathos of the wounded or dead child is reabsorbed into the drama of young U.S. soldiers under duress. An inherited discourse of masculine performance, the sedimented memory of past war representation, gives way to a confessional mode of vulnerable youth lost, as the song goes, in a wilderness of pain.

As I have discussed in this chapter, the practice of embedment—which has been discontinued by the U.S. military—carried strengths as well as limitations. It allowed photographers and journalists an extended and unusual degree of access to combat soldiers in their practices of daily life. Yet the policy necessarily circumscribed the

Sergeant Rougle learning of his new assignment, Rock Avalanche, where he will meet his death. *Restrepo*, directed by Tim Hetherington and Sebastian Junger, 2010. Produced by Tim Hetherington, Sebastian Junger, and Nick Quested.

potential for criticism as well as the possibility of narrating an alternate perspective. Although I feel the body of work produced by Hetherington and Junger in the Korengal Valley manifests subtleties of voice and perspective that undercut any explicit cinematic identification with the soldiers or endorsement of their acts, other writers have found the work of Hetherington and Junger, while embedded with Battle Company, to be collusive with the U.S. military project in Afghanistan.

Viewing the issue of embedded journalism as one of representation, however—of representing a reality that exists independently of the camera, a reality that the optical apparatus records and represents in celluloid or digital form—may not be the most productive way to approach this issue. As a thought experiment, I suggest that the question might be framed in a different way: How does the battlefield itself change because of the camera? How does war change under the camera's gaze? Can the issues associated with embedment be part of a larger set of issues concerning the changed environment the presence of the camera creates? In a recent discussion, Francesco Casetti stated that the camera on the battlefield changes the field itself: the battlefield ought to be thought of as a mediascape. Once a camera is in an environment, he asserted, the environment as such

OP Restrepo toward the end of Battle Company's fifteen-month deployment. *Restrepo,* directed by Tim Hetherington and Sebastian Junger, 2010. Produced by Tim Hetherington, Sebastian Junger, and Nick Quested.

becomes cinematic—the camera functions, in his view, not as an optical medium but as an environmental medium.[19]

The embedment of the photographer Hetherington and the writer Junger for a year with Battle Company would seem to illustrate this point, with the camera becoming an intrinsic part of the environment and hence, perhaps changing that environment. At the most basic level, the ubiquitous presence of the camera during the long stretch of embedment brings the question of performance to the foreground: to what extent did the soldiers of Battle Company perform as soldiers for the camera? Did inherited visual and gestural codes of soldiery, cued by the camera, shape a style of self-presentation in the outpost and on patrol? Following from this, we can ask whether the Afghan elders of the loya jirga—the council of elders described above—also performed their roles as elders for the camera? Did they speak or withhold speech because of the camera? Moving beyond the effects on behavior that the presence of the camera almost certainly entails, the larger role and provenance of the images of *Restrepo, Infidel, Into the Korengal,* and *Sleeping Soldiers* might be imagined in a different way, not as recording reality as such but as opening a dialogue with other images of war. Scenes of trauma, of soldiers sleeping, of men gearing up for combat, of mourning, have extensive visual historical antecedents. If Casetti is right, the presence of the camera in the field of war transforms the battlespace into a cinematic space, a mediascape, contributing to and evoking a network of visual frames that have come to define war for the viewer—and perhaps for the soldiers themselves.

The works I discuss in this chapter bring into heightened relief certain questions of war representation that are particular to the war in Afghanistan, a conflict that at first glance appears to be unique in U.S. history—what seemed like an endless siege with no obvious strategic or tactical purpose, and with almost no visibility in the wider U.S. culture. Nonetheless, these works summon the sedimentary history of conflict photography and film. In many ways, the shift in genre codes that I have attempted to describe in this volume can be sensed here as an attempt to graft the familiar topoi of war representation onto a deeply unfamiliar narrative of a war without a mission, without obvious agency, and without a sense of conclusion or resolution. Maybe it is too soon to map these images into a larger constellation of contemporary war, to connect these scenes of trauma, loss, and violence into an overarching cultural script. Or maybe, as the work of Hetherington and Junger suggests, the wars in Afghanistan and Iraq are still being continued on other stages, in the haunted psyches of a generation of soldiers as well as in the domestic spaces of U.S. daily life, where the mentality of war now seems to preside and a sense of embattlement has taken hold.

CHAPTER 6

AMERICAN PASTORAL

American Sniper

TWO SCENES, one at the beginning of the film and one near the end, create a chilling formal rhyme that underlines the larger patterns of violence threaded through *American Sniper* (2014). In the opening sequence, Petty Officer Chris Kyle (played by Bradley Cooper), the sniper of the film's title, is seen at the start of his first assignment in Iraq, watching over a city road as a convoy of marines is about to drive through. A burqa-clad woman and a young boy walk slowly out of a doorway. Kyle is on alert—there is something about her way of walking that seems odd. As he watches them through his sniper's scope, the woman reaches inside her robe and takes out a large grenade. She hands it to the boy, who begins running toward the convoy in order to get close enough to fling the weapon. As he lifts the grenade for the throw, the film cuts away from the action to a series of flashback scenes of Kyle's boyhood—his first hunting experience; his violent rescue of his brother, who is being beaten by a bully; the lesson his father imparts at the dinner table concerning the wolves, the sheep, and the sheepdog who protects the sheep. We then return to the scene in Iraq, as Kyle pulls the trigger. As we watch through the scope, the young boy collapses, a bullet wound in the middle of his chest. The woman, perhaps his mother, then rushes to him, picks up the grenade, and tries to hurl it at the convoy herself. Kyle shoots her as well, causing the grenade to fall short. His first two shots as a sniper in Iraq have thus been directed at a young boy and his mother—actions that may have saved ten marines, he is told, but that clearly exact a psychic toll.

Chris Kyle, in his suburban home, at the end of the film. *American Sniper*, directed by Clint Eastwood, 2014. Produced by Clint Eastwood, Robert Lorenz, Andrew Lazar, Bradley Cooper, and Peter Morgan.

Fast-forward to the last sequence of the film. The setting is Kyle's suburban home, a sunlit interior in the middle of the day. The scene begins with the camera focusing in close-up on a large revolver, pointed into the living room, as Kyle walks silently through the house. Framed at waist height, we also see the rodeo belt he had won in a contest earlier in the film. The camera takes in Kyle's young daughter, who smiles and giggles at him, and then his young son, also smiling and playing a video game. Kyle finds his wife in the kitchen, stops in the doorway, cocks the revolver, and speaks. She turns to him, laughing.

The nightmare quality of this scene, in which a pistol cocked and seemingly aimed at a loving family seems to be a "normal" form of behavior, eliciting smiles and laughter rather than terror, captures the complex and devastating critique of violence in American culture that Clint Eastwood sets forth in this film. The violence of war haunts the American dreamscape, the film suggests, as it draws a series of parallels between the war in Iraq and the culture of violence that has penetrated U.S. domestic life. Framing a story of psychological damage, PTSD, and moral injury through the prism of the autobiography of Chris Kyle, who was given the nickname "Legend" for his prowess as a sniper, the film explores the dark paradox of war, in which Kyle's courage and commitment as a soldier—he signed on for four tours of duty in Iraq—leads directly to increasing instability and brooding obsession at home, an instability that devolves into auditory hallucinations, paranoia, and rage. In *American Sniper*, the concept of productive pathology, which I discussed above, finds its clarified expression, as the character displays both consummate skill on the battlefield, an implacable singleness of purpose, and a kind of frozen withdrawal from the world when he is home between tours. As Jonna Eagle has written, Kyle is portrayed both as lethal agent and as suffering victim, "psychically burdened by the very weapons that render him deadly."[1]

These two distant places, the battlefield in Iraq and the U.S. homeland, as the film makes clear, are not separate or distinct. Formally, the work is dominated by crosscutting, suturing scenes of combat in Iraq and ordinary life in the United States. Twice, Kyle and his wife, Taya (Sienna Miller), are speaking on the phone when a firefight breaks out, the sounds of shots and battlefield mayhem erupting through the ether as Taya tries to talk with Chris. The terror—and sometimes outright horror—of Kyle's experiences in Iraq redefine the most intimate moments of their lives together, the moments revolving around Taya's pregnancies and the birth of their two children. The interpenetration of one realm by another in the moment-to-moment unfolding of the story, the gluing together of the ordinary scenes and spaces of American life and the violent aggression of war, touches on an area of war representation that has seldom been explored in American film and has a particular salience in the present day.

In this chapter, I explore a theme that I have considered, in outline form, throughout this book—the diffusion of the emotions, gestures, and mentality of war into daily American life—a theme that is made explicit in *American Sniper*. The violence that permeates the film is rendered boldly in the scenes set in Iraq, in which brutality, atrocity, and death are given full audition. The feral violence of war, however, is portrayed as also living just beneath the surface of the U.S. suburban world, a pastoral realm of dogs, children, and barbecues. In the film's depiction of the character of Chris Kyle, the shadow world that the returning combat soldier inhabits comes into full view, a subjective reality defined by threat and guilt.

In its complex engagement with PTSD and moral injury, its dramatization of the warping of personality and perception caused by war, *American Sniper* succeeds in embedding a pointed social and historical critique of the culture of war within an empathetic treatment of the soldiers who serve. The film underlines their commitment and purpose while exposing war's destructive effects on the soldiers themselves, their families, and importantly, the Iraqi families the U.S. soldiers encounter.[2]

The plot of the film is recursive, introducing Kyle's early life story in the suspended moments between training his scope on the young Iraqi boy with the grenade and pulling the trigger. At several points, the film returns to a kind of repetition and variation of the pattern set out in the opening. In the first set of subjective flashbacks, for example, in the split seconds before he pulls the trigger, Kyle is seen being anointed by his father after he successfully shoots his first deer—he has "a gift" for marksmanship, his father says, and a responsibility to protect those less strong. As if the successive repetition of a rule or a routine were his only mode for confronting the present, the character follows this principle almost programmatically.

Later, the film sketches his young adulthood in a series of vignettes, depicting him riding broncos, winning rodeo competitions, and highlighting his affection for his younger brother. In these short scenes, the film paints the character and his life in the narrative style that Gerard Genette calls the frequentative mode: events that are portrayed once stand in for a series of typical events, in this case, a regular order of experiences consisting of rodeos, beer, and rowdy nights.[3] Then 9/11 occurs.

Kyle quickly enlists in the Navy SEALs and endures a harrowing training regimen. His skill as a sharpshooter is soon recognized. Before he deploys to Iraq, however, he embarks on a fast-paced romance with a young woman he meets at a bar near the base, Taya, every bit his match for wit and physical attractiveness. From this point forward, in several key scenes, the focal perspective is split between the two characters.

In Iraq, Kyle's superior skill as a sniper is demonstrated in a montage of quickly executed kills. His fame in the U.S. military and among the insurgents travels fast and far: the insurgents soon issue a wanted poster for him, promising a lavish reward for his death. Despite the danger, he is not content to sit in relative safety on a rooftop to look out for threats; he insists on joining the marines in their door-to-door searches. In these street-level encounters, Kyle finds himself breaking into family homes, intimidating children, women, and older men, and essentially violating the domestic worlds of families who are not unlike the one he and Taya hope to establish in the States. Moreover, in what increasingly develops into a mirror-world doubling, Kyle is shadowed by an enemy sniper, a man the soldiers have named Mustafa, who seems to be present at every skirmish Kyle is involved in. In one scene, Kyle is pinned down by this doppelgänger and barely manages to escape.

On his various returns to the States between tours, he is plagued with demons. He will not leave his house and barely communicates with his wife, who is trying to keep their marriage together and raise a family. The traumatic effects of combat, which he assigns to his grief over the men he could not protect, are clearly etched on his features and in his figure behavior. He rails against the indifference of the public to the war, angered that people can go about their ordinary lives while soldiers are dying in Iraq and Afghanistan. At home between tours, he wears the same stained baseball cap as when he is on duty in Iraq, where he turns the brim backward before he sets up in his sniper's position. At one point, after he returns from his fourth deployment, he is portrayed staring at a TV screen that has been turned off, as the sounds of war are heard on the soundtrack.

In the final act of the film, Kyle experiences a frightening breakdown, after which he finally agrees to talk to a VA therapist. The therapist suggests that if he still wants to help his fellow soldiers, he might speak with those who are in the hospital for treatment. From this point in the narrative, Kyle is moving toward emotional and mental health: his involvement with other veterans suffering from devastating physical and mental injuries proves to be powerfully therapeutic. A series of short, affectionate scenes with his daughter, his son, and his wife steer the film toward its conclusion. A happy resolution is in view. Taya tells Chris how proud she is of him and compliments him on what a great father and husband he has become. Then she sees a hollow-eyed man in their driveway, waiting for Chris by his truck—a troubled former soldier whom Kyle has arranged to take to the shooting range. In the last shot of the narrative, she watches out the door as they drive off together. A brief title then comes on the screen, stating that Chris Kyle was killed that day by a fellow soldier he was trying to help.

THE CHILD IN WAR

Images of children under threat appear throughout *American Sniper,* recurring in several scenes set in Iraq and in the States, and stamping each of the film's main acts. As I have argued elsewhere in this book, the child as victim and target of war forms a central motif in the films I consider, one that summons complex emotions of sympathy, fear, and guilt in the protagonists while also shifting to Western characters the pathos associated with the vulnerable or wounded innocent. Examples can be found in scenes in *The Hurt Locker* (2008), *Eye in the Sky* (2015), *Restrepo* (2010), in the form of wounded tribal children, and *A Private War* (2018), with the dying Palestinian girl and the Syrian child whose last moments are broadcast on CNN. In each of these works, the image of the child victim lingers, haunting the main characters. Moreover, in each of these films, the pathos conventionally associated with the child in war, the emotions that would ordinarily attach to the child victim, are transferred instead to the Western protagonist, whose guilt and suffering is rendered at length. A curious psychological double identity occurs in these scenes, in which the protagonists serving as the agents of war, or those reporting on war, wear the face of the victims of war.

The repeated images of the vulnerable child in *American Sniper,* however, are distinct from what we have seen in other films. At the beginning of the work, for example, Kyle's younger brother is shown being beaten by a schoolyard bully; Kyle rescues his brother with force, violently overpowering the much larger boy. Later, just after his daughter is born, Kyle visits the hospital neonatal clinic and sees that his newly born child is crying; the nurse is tending to another infant. Kyle can scarcely contain himself as he pounds on the thick glass wall trying to get the nurse's attention. And toward the end of the film, at a backyard barbecue, Kyle's son is shown playing keep-away with the family dog. When the dog gets the boy on the ground, playfully tugging at his hoodie, Kyle responds with frightening rage.

In the combat scenes set in Iraq, however, the image of the child in war takes on more sinister characteristics. At two different points in the film, Kyle is confronted with a child wielding a weapon. In the first instance, as briefly discussed above, Kyle peers through his scope as the young Iraqi boy with a grenade is about to hurl it at a convoy of American soldiers. The sniper pauses to make certain the boy is going to throw the grenade, and then shoots him. His careful observation reads as deliberateness, calculation, and finally reluctant acceptance of what he must do. The second time he confronts a child with a weapon, late into his third deployment, the scene carries a different charge. Kyle has just dispatched an Iraqi gunman wielding a large grenade launcher. The heavy piece falls to the ground. A young boy approaches and tries to pick up the unwieldy weapon. As Kyle watches the boy struggle with the heavy ordnance, his finger on the trigger, he is consumed by dread, whispering to himself, "Don't pick up the weapon, don't pick it up!" The long, agonizing scene plays out as an ordeal, an emotional rack and screw, as Kyle is clearly at a breaking point. When the boy abandons the weapon and takes off running, Kyle cries with relief.

In these scenes, which function as dramatic crescendos, Kyle's image of himself, the compass of his world and his position in it, is first threatened and then breaks down. The orderly, pastoral universe mapped by his father—where the sheep, the wolves, and the sheepdog exist in a kind of fixed and balanced equilibrium—is thrown into disarray in the very first scene, where Kyle, confronted with the necessity of killing a child and his mother, must assume the role of the wolf, as well as that of protector of the troops. Depicting combat as a carousel of vulnerable, victimized, and predatory figures, with each type continually circling into view, the film propels Kyle into a series of tense scenes where the roles and positions unexpectedly change. Even the children are revealed to be dangerous. Reminiscent in some ways of Sigmund Freud's well-known deconstruction of the fantasy "A Child Is Being Beaten," the identities of the agents of violence and the victims of violence are not constant; the roles change as the combat situations unfold.[4]

The imagery of the child victim, and the twisting and shifting of symbolic roles that it generates, reaches its apotheosis in a scene near the middle of the film. A sadist nicknamed "the Butcher," a villain of outsized proportions, serves in the film as an enforcer for the insurgent leader Abu Musab al-Zarqawi. The Butcher, a fictional creation, has a reputation for severing body parts from his victims and saving them; he is also known for using an electric drill as a torture and execution device. During his initial deployment, Kyle leads a team that is charged with finding and dispatching al-Zarqawi, who is hiding somewhere in the city. After breaking into a neighborhood house, Kyle aggressively confronts the father of a family, as his wife and children cower in the background. Roughly insisting that the man talk to him, Kyle extracts information about the Butcher, including his actual name. Soon after, the team of marines returns to the neighborhood, planning to pay the man for his good information. En route in a Humvee, Kyle takes a call from Taya, who has phoned to tell him that she has just found out that the child they are expecting is a boy.

Directly after Taya relays this information to Kyle, we see the expert sniper, Mustafa, take aim and shoot the driver of the Humvee. The vehicle crashes and the insurgent sniper begins picking off soldiers. As Taya listens to the battle through the cell phone, Kyle is forced to take cover, leaving his phone behind. The film cuts rapidly among Taya, standing at the entrance to the hospital; Mustafa, in cool control of the battle zone at his sniper's post; and Kyle, keeping low, barely evading Mustafa's shots. The Butcher then appears, dragging the young son of the Iraqi informant outside into the square. As the mother and father plead with him, the Butcher applies the drill to the boy's head and then kills the father, saying that if the villagers talk to the soldiers they will die with the soldiers.

The adrenalized emotion of the scene is ramped up by the near stasis of the figures. The editing ricochets from the horrifying Grand Guignol unfolding in the square; to the impassive face of Mustafa, sighting his targets; to the scrabbling impotence of Kyle as he tries to lift his head to get a shot; to the anguished face of Taya, listening on the phone. The melodramatic terror of the young boy's execution is projected directly into the heart of the U.S. homeland. It is as if we see the scene through the imaginative perspective of Taya. Once more, as in the case of several other films I have discussed, the pathos and tragedy of the young boy and his family, the Iraqi victims of the attack, is transferred to the Western characters, in this case, to Taya, who serves as the scene's focalizer.

What has also occurred, however, is another rotation of roles. Kyle's insistence on breaking into the neighborhood home, his determination to extract information from the father of the family, exposes the man, leading directly to the torture and death of his son, followed by his own death. At the exact point in the narrative when Kyle is presented with the news of his own son, soon to be born, he witnesses the death of the son of the Iraqi informant—a killing that is, at some level, his fault.

In a scene filled with melodramatic intensity, the film embeds a series of mirror structures: a son who is killed and a son who is about to be born, a father who dies and a father to be. And in the character of Taya, the mirroring is made explicit: like the Iraqi mother in the scene, she is frantic, nearly doubled over, suffused with grief and worry. The heightened dramatic tension of the sequence, its Goya-like horror, to some degree conceals its most salient point—that the violence of war spreads far beyond the battlefield, to the intimate lives of everyone involved, especially the noncombatants.

"IT WAS THAT LETTER THAT KILLED MARC"

As the film progresses, Kyle establishes a close friendship with two members of the SEAL team, Biggles (Jake McDorman) and Marc (Luke Grimes), the team leader. The two men present contrasting character types familiar from numerous war films, including *Saving Private Ryan* (1998), *Full Metal Jacket* (1987), and *Letters from Iwo Jima* (2006). Biggles performs as the jokester, jesting with Kyle about his prowess as a sniper, nicknaming him "Legend" and providing an easygoing comradeship. Marc, for his part, serves as wry philosopher. A former seminarian, he is cool, reflective, and somewhat detached from the rest of the team's exuberant style. Both of Kyle's friends are killed in battle.

Narratives of war are distinguished by the remarkable stability of their conventions, which have remained in place, more or less unchanged, from the time of the *Iliad*. Despite vast historical, technological, and aesthetic shifts over the course of more than two millennia, the core narrative events and scenes of the war narrative have largely remained consistent. One of the most symbolically potent conventions of war cinema is the scene of mourning for a fallen comrade. The representation of battlefield death and its aftermath, in scenes of mourning and burial, often provides a revelatory moment, a nodal point, in which the emotional vectors of the war story intersect with codes of cultural performance and historical memory. The wider significance of war for the culture and the period is often crystallized in these scenes. In the contemporary war film, however, such scenes are often nothing but a remnant. In *The Hurt Locker, Zero Dark Thirty* (2012), and *Restrepo*, for example, rituals of mourning are notably muted, if they are depicted at all. Rather, the death of a major character in these works is registered quietly, as a diffuse melancholy that settles over the film. The absent mourning and burial scenes of these works may be a distant echo of the films of World War I, where no one remained to tell the story or cared to remember.[5]

American Sniper, in contrast to the majority of Iraq and Afghanistan war films, gives full weight to the convention of the mourning and burial scene. Evoking genre memory, the film appears, at least at first glance, to revert to an older code of military and social ritual. Two such scenes are enacted in the film—the funeral and burial of SEAL team leader Marc, killed in an ambush in Iraq, and the funeral of the biographical Chris Kyle—the latter consisting of documentary footage added to the film after Kyle was killed in the United States by a fellow veteran suffering from PTSD. (I address the second funeral and mourning scene, which concludes the film, at the end of the chapter.)

The first burial scene follows directly from the fatal ambush in Iraq. Soon after Marc is shot, the film cuts to the interior of a military plane transporting five flag-draped caskets back to the States. Kyle and a couple of other men accompany the remains. As the men sit silently on the plane, the sound of a woman's trembling voice is asynchronously superimposed over the scene. She enunciates the words in a slow, formal rhythm: "Glory is something some men chase and others find themselves stumbling upon, not expecting to find it." The film then cuts to Marc's burial ceremony, with Kyle and Taya in attendance, as the speaking woman, evidently Marc's mother, continues her recitation, now on camera, reading a letter from her son. "My question is when does glory fade away and become a wrongful crusade?" A cut to Kyle and Taya occurs here. "Or an unjustified means which consumes one completely. I've seen war and I've seen death." On the word "death," a navy honor guard begins their salute, presenting arms, taking aim, and firing three rounds into the air. At the sound of the shots, Taya flinches; Marc's mother sobs and shakes her head slightly, as if rejecting the salute. The film then cuts to the bugler playing "Taps," to the folding of the flag, to the presentation of the flag to a younger woman, perhaps Marc's wife. In close-up, Taya slowly lifts her gaze to Kyle's impassive face. He marks his farewell by pounding his SEAL insignia into the coffin, where it joins the insignias of other team members.

The discordant notes of dissent within a solemn ritual meant to mold consensus around the value of sacrifice for nation has been reinforced by the scene's visual accents, in particular the close-ups of Taya and Marc's mother. Moreover, the themes of the traditional commemoration for the fallen soldier are undercut by the written words of the man being honored, even as the ritualized gestures, the choreographed movements, and the sounding of "Taps" are played out. On the ride home, Taya insists on hearing from Chris what he thought of the letter Marc had sent to his mother two weeks before. Chris responds, "It wasn't the ambush, it was that letter killed Marc. He let go, and he paid the price for it." Kyle's response is punctuated by his wary glances into the rearview mirror, where he sees a van that seems to be following too closely, as daily life now harbors visible and invisible threats. The intrusion of doubt and ambivalence into the fraternal world of the SEALs, instantiated here by Marc's letter, constitutes one such threat; Taya's skepticism represents another. Far from serving as a symbolic enactment of loss and collective renewal, the burial scene has here become a confession of doubt and a form of penance, in which the words "wrongful crusade" and "unjustified means" mark a very different perspective on war than that taken by Kyle.

MUSTAFA

Following Marc's funeral, Kyle returns to Iraq for his fourth deployment, motivated, it seems, not by patriotic commitment but by a sense of unfinished business—the insurgent sniper Mustafa. The character is presented in the film as a dark double to Kyle; dressed in black, with a black kerchief tied behind his head, he is depicted in several scenes preparing for his assignments, moving into a secure position from which to shoot, taking aim, and dispatching American soldiers with ease. Unlike Kyle, however, he is not seen in the company of other fighters; his spotters in the city alert him via cell phone to the movements and locations of American troops. In one scene, Mustafa is pictured "at home," in rooms he shares with a young woman, presumably his wife, and an infant. As Mustafa spins a large bullet on the table in front of him, we view a reward poster with Chris Kyle's image on it. When the bullet stops spinning, it is pointed directly at Mustafa.

The throwback formula of two gunslingers destined to face off on a dusty street has a long history in the Western genre, of course, including Eastwood's own films, and a short history in war cinema as well. The most immediate reference point may be Jean-Jacques Annaud's *Enemy at the Gates* (2001), which is dominated by a fictional duel between a German and a Russian sniper during the siege of Leningrad during World War II. Similarly, in *American Sniper*, Mustafa is present during each of Kyle's four deployments and develops a legendary reputation in his own right. As a marksman, he is portrayed as an equal to Chris Kyle—an Olympic gold medalist who competed for Syria, as we discover from a photo on the wall of his dwelling. He is also portrayed as a father and a husband, further linking him with Kyle. In the asymmetrical warfare of Iraq, the contest of Mustafa and Kyle creates a kind of symmetry, where the abilities of the two gunmen are evenly matched and their domestic lives, the film suggests, comparable.

During Kyle's fourth deployment, he has an opportunity to take a shot at Mustafa, although the distance of 2,100 yards would seem to make contact impossible. Moreover, a sandstorm is blowing in. The commanding officer, fearing the gunshot will alert the insurgents to the Americans' presence, insists that Kyle not risk it; several times, the officer in command tells Kyle not to shoot, that to do so will put the entire team in danger. Kyle ignores him, sets himself, and fires a bullet that the camera follows in slow motion to its target.

A dramatic array of shot sizes and camera movements set this scene apart, including drone images from on high, footage from a racing U.S. helicopter, and extreme, static close-ups. The centerpiece of the scene, the kernel around which the sequence builds, however, is the extraordinary exchange of matching close-ups pairing Kyle and Mustafa, each of whom is shown sighting their targets, an exchange rendered in dramatic portraiture shots that build in size and intensity as the action unfolds. The rhyming movements and parallel actions of the two shooters, as each sniper composes himself, releases the safety, and pulls the trigger, and the matching views

Chris Kyle, lining up a shot. *American Sniper,* directed by Clint Eastwood, 2014. Produced by Clint Eastwood, Robert Lorenz, Andrew Lazar, Bradley Cooper, and Peter Morgan.

Mustafa, the Syrian sniper, Chris Kyle's dark doppelgänger. *American Sniper,* directed by Clint Eastwood, 2014. Produced by Clint Eastwood, Robert Lorenz, Andrew Lazar, Bradley Cooper, and Peter Morgan.

through both snipers' scopes, as first Mustafa hits his target—a U.S. soldier—and then, a few minutes later, as Kyle hits his, suggest that the two characters can be seen as two halves of the same figure.

In the Vietnam War movie *The Deer Hunter* (1978), the "one shot" exalted by the film's characters as the acme of righteous violence—tragically enacted in its concluding scene of Russian roulette—is both a manifestation of an ideal and an ironic marker, a karmic summary, of war's losses. It is a clear reference point for *American Sniper.* The suicide that darkens the ending of the earlier film is not far from view in the film's portrayal of Chris Kyle, even in the scene that most emphatically demonstrates his prowess. Although he rightly maintains that Mustafa "had eyes on our guys," his one shot reveals the

U.S. soldiers' position and, as the officer had warned, insurgents quickly swarm them. As the sandstorm begins to build, a protracted firefight breaks out. Overwhelmed by insurgents, with his team running out of ammunition, unable to be quickly extracted from the area, the team leader calls for a missile strike on their own position, saying he doesn't want to be "dragged through the street." As the helicopter armed with the missile approaches, Kyle calls Taya on his cell phone and tells her, as he breaks down, that he is "ready to come home." As in the previous scene, Taya is crosscut into the middle of the firefight, as she listens to Kyle over the furor of the battle. As we watch the missile's trajectory from the perspective of the pilot, the wind of the sandstorm causes the shot to miss. The exfiltration team finally arrives, and with the blowing sand almost completely blotting out the camera's view the unit is rescued.

The scene of Kyle's "impossible shot" has been criticized for its triumphal assertion of dominance and its atavistic elevation of individual combat. Roger Stahl, for example, understands the moment as a crystallized expression of what he calls the "weaponized gaze" that has, in his view, dominated American culture for the past thirty years. The sequence and the film overall, he argues, consistently fuses the spectator's gaze with the viewfinder of the weapon, be it the drone or the sniper scope. The optical collaboration that results reinforces identification with the character of Chris Kyle, thus positioning the spectator as complicit with a generalized assent to the war. Enlarging this point, Stahl argues that the American spectator, over the past thirty years—since the Gulf War—has in effect become a participant in the military apparatus, secured through an optical identification that is continuously renewed in media coverage, films, and video games. Seduced into an alignment with the military gaze, the American spectator is lured into an uncritical acceptance of what Stahl sees as the dominant narrative of American history, centered on imperialism and aggression.

In the impossible-shot sequence of *American Sniper,* this identification, for Stahl, attains its most direct expression. Kyle's relentless, impossibly accurate marksmanship becomes a symbolic resolution, rehabilitating a nation wounded to its core by the terror attacks of 9/11: "Seized by a mystical moment of intuition rivalling only David's impossible hit on Goliath, Kyle pulls the trigger and successfully takes Mustafa out. . . . We zoom in on Mustafa, marking his eye for annihilation, even as he peers through his own scope."[6]

Stahl's reading of the film, which is highly critical, emphasizes the point-of-view shots in the film, especially those through the sniper's scope, which he takes as a synecdoche for the whole battery of optical weaponry that has been such a prominent aspect of actual war since the invention of photography, a critical position first set out by Paul Virilio.[7] Where I disagree with Stahl's analysis of the film is in his blanket understanding of the work as a celebration of U.S. state violence through its principal warrior avatar, Chris Kyle. This work's complex mode of address, in which violence as the default setting in American history and culture is held up to scrutiny and critique but rendered in a form that gives credence to the patriotism and bravery of soldiers at war, is not considered in Stahl's analysis.

Chris Kyle's shooting of Mustafa, an act he commits despite a direct order to stand down, forces the commanding officer to call in a suicide strike on the U.S. position, an action that will certainly kill the entire company in addition to the insurgents attacking the building. Although the slow-motion transit of the bullet from Kyle's rifle has been taken as the signature shot of the film, the much larger bullet—the missile fired from the U.S. helicopter, aimed at the company of U.S. soldiers—might be considered its symbolic counterpart. The mirror construction that dominates the film here returns with a vengeance, as the U.S. military has turned its guns on itself.

HOMECOMING / THE WOUNDS OF WAR

Directly after Kyle has been exfiltrated from the firefight—a scene that ends with a fifteen-second brownout from the sandstorm—the film recommences with Kyle seated in a nearly empty bar. Taya calls and tells him she has heard he was on a flight. Asking if he is in Germany or something, she learns that Kyle is "stateside" and that he "just needed a minute." He had been in Iraq, on his fourth deployment, for the last nine months.

Rather than the awkward, difficult, or tearful homecoming that is part of the standard syntax of war cinema, the film cuts immediately from the scene in the bar to a shot of Kyle sitting in a chair in the living room. As noted above, he appears to be watching TV as the sounds of war are heard on the soundtrack, including those of helicopters, children screaming, and explosions. As the camera circles around him, the TV is shown to be dark: Kyle is staring at his own reflection. Called out of his reverie by Taya, who asks him to join her at a neighborhood barbecue, he erupts in a killing rage as the family dog begins pulling on his son's hoodie; he is stopped in his assault on the dog only by Taya's shouts. He then visits a VA hospital and speaks with a psychologist, who recommends talking with the other wounded veterans in the hospital.

American Sniper paints the VA hospital and the wounded veterans who live and meet there in a relaxed, naturalistic way, with none of the lurid expressionism that has attended these scenes in Vietnam War films such as *Born on the Fourth of July*. The veterans, despite their injuries, seem talkative and cheerful, and somewhat adjusted to now wholly transformed bodies and lives. One soldier, whom Kyle jokes with about his reputed boot collection, gives Kyle a fine pair of Western boots, a warm gesture that may also be a foreshadowing—the gift recalls, however obliquely, the boot exchange in *All Quiet on the Western Front* (1930), where a pair of excellent boots is passed from friend to friend as each, in turn, is killed. During this short, somewhat happier segment of the film, Kyle is seen reestablishing his bond with his son, his daughter, and his wife, and seemingly moving toward health. The demons of war—Kyle had been deployed "in country" for over one thousand days—seem for the moment to be at bay.

In the final scene, however, as Kyle stalks through the suburban house playacting a Western gunman, the film resumes a complex double voicing. Taya receives his performance with happy approval, as a sign that he has returned to health. The violence implied by the gun and the order to "drop your drawers, little lady" has moved into the imaginative realm, where it can be performed, seemingly without cost. But the sinister figure of the veteran waiting in the driveway for Kyle gives a different accent to this scene. As Taya looks out the kitchen door, the man stares back at her. The camera returns to Taya as Chris greets the man and gives him the plan for the day. In five increasingly close shots, she silently watches their exchange. The narrative of the film ends with a slow fade on Taya's face as she closes the kitchen door.

Taya, Chris Kyle's wife, looking at Chris for the last time. *American Sniper*, directed by Clint Eastwood, 2014. Produced by Clint Eastwood, Robert Lorenz, Andrew Lazar, Bradley Cooper, and Peter Morgan.

In Stahl's reading of the film, the pastoral provides a key interpretive frame, which he describes in terms of Michel Foucault's discussion of the pastoral as a model of patriarchal obedience.[8] The enunciation of this theme by Kyle's father early in the film—in the analogy of the sheep, the sheepdog, and the wolves—can be understood in this way, as the assertion of a regulatory order, a system of control. And toward the close of the film, images of nature, animals, and the bucolic American life abound, as if a regular order, a stable world, could once again be found. Chris introduces his son to hunting, in a scene bathed in autumnal light, and takes his daughter to a ranch to admire a white horse, frisking in the sun. The pastoral's power as an allegory of order, however, is no sooner rendered than it is overturned. The roles described in the pastoral, as discussed above, are not stable—the protector becomes the prey, and even those who need protection (the vulnerable, the wounded, and the psychically damaged) can take on a predatory role. As the film informs us with a closing graphic title, "Chris Kyle was killed that day by a veteran he was trying to help."

CODA

In the film's second mourning and funeral sequence, which consists of documentary footage and still photographs of the biographical Chris Kyle's funeral, the iconography of nation and patriotism looms large. The funeral cortege, a large escort of police motorcycles and squad cars, proceeds solemnly along the highways leading into Dallas, roadways that are lined with people paying their respects to Kyle, and crossed by bridges crowded with people waving flags and holding signs. As the procession moves into Cowboys Stadium, a series of still shots replaces the moving images, featuring a uniformed bugler, an honor guard of SEALs in formal wear, and photographs of the real-life Chris and Taya. A full choir, hushed but audible, back the trumpet solo that accompanies the scene. One of the last images of the film is a photo of a soldier in full combat gear, offering a salute, with the sun setting in the distance and a flag flying. The scene reads almost as an apotheosis.

The two mourning scenes depicted in the film seem to stand at antipodes to each other. The message of dissent that rang loudly in Marc's funeral is nowhere to be found in the documentary images of the final salute to Kyle. Instead, the closing scene marshals an array of patriotic images, sounds, and symbols. Viewed in a broader, intertextual light, Eastwood's use of real-life footage here might be compared to the coda of Eastwood's *Flags of Our Fathers* (2006), a film that set out to demystify the discourse of heroism that pervaded the Seventh War Bond tour of World War II, an instance of manufactured patriotism that might be said to characterize American war culture as a whole. Snapshots and film footage of the actual American soldiers whose stories were dramatized in the film are rendered in a lengthy commemorative montage. Shots of ordinary GIs posing for the camera, running into the ocean to swim, and the like function as a closing counterweight, where life's quotidian pleasures are set against the constructed patriotic fervor that had distorted the lives of the men celebrated as flag raisers at the Battle of Iwo Jima. And in *Letters from Iwo Jima*, the counterpart to *Flags of Our Fathers*, Eastwood also employs a coda. A work that undercuts the Japanese wartime belief in the transcendent value of dying for the emperor and the sacred homeland, the ending shots of *Letters from Iwo Jima* emphasize ordinary emotions. Cutting from the closing scenes of the World War II story to an archaeological dig on the island some decades later, a bag of undelivered letters is found. As they are spilled out and cascade to the floor, a montage of voices suggesting those of the soldier–authors, long dead, suffuses the soundtrack. In both of these earlier war films, fabricated patriotism and the cultural exploitation of the soldier's death as sacrifice is held up to scrutiny. In both codas, a seemingly prosaic, redemptive ending stands apart from the powerful critiques that shape each film as a whole.

The coda of *American Sniper*, however, carries a different semiotic valence, providing a kind of concrete instantiation, a documentary testament to the persistence of a concept of nation that remains in place, and has indeed been reinforced, in the twenty-first century, in which war, and the rhetoric and symbolism of soldiery, claim an outsized symbolic importance. By the end of *American Sniper*, it is clear that the symbols of war as the emblems of patriotism have come detached from their referents. Portrayed as a soldier who has embraced an older vision of the American mission, Kyle has ardently subscribed to the traditional narratives of rescue, brotherhood, and sacrifice. He is killed, however, not by an enemy combatant but by a distressed former marine, another dark doppelgänger. Here, the poignancy of the film, and its tragic meaning, comes into focus. In the ceremonial tribute that closes the film, the reality of war, the moral, physical, and psychic decay it brings about, as well as the devastation it causes to ordinary people in both near and distant places, is set to one side. The iconography of military ritual, instead, dominates the stage, as if to acknowledge the fact that the symbols and narratives of war still hold an imaginative potency, despite all lessons to the contrary. Although *American Sniper* powerfully anatomizes the psychic and social costs of war in the twenty-first century, the beliefs and illusions that sustain the mentalité of the contemporary period are here given voice as well.

In this chapter, I have argued that *American Sniper* performs an immanent critique of war and the culture of violence that pervades American life, all while embedding its critical perspective in a form that gives credence to the commitment and sense of purpose of ordinary soldiers. In its use of genre conventions, the film employs a complex double voice: the spectacle and drama of combat is rendered in a familiar cinematic language of kinetic intensity, and then reframed, through patterns of doubling and reversal, to reveal the costs of war's violence, which in the words of Kyle's friend Marc "consumes one completely." This complex double voicing has led to an extremely mixed critical response, with many writers seizing on the actions and words of the main character as a full-blown endorsement of the war in Iraq, despite Eastwood's repeated statements that the film is anti-war.[9]

A more subtle understanding of the film can be found in the work of writers such as Vito Zagarrio and James Curnow, who each argue that the biographical source material of the work—the memoir written by the historical Chris Kyle—would make impossible an explicitly anti-war statement on the part of the film. Zagarrio, in particular, notes that such an overt anti-war perspective would betray the convictions of the author, whose full-throated support of the American bloodletting in Iraq is explicit throughout the book. In a wide-ranging essay, he links the film to the critical perspective Eastwood displays in works such as *Gran Torino* (2008), *A Perfect World* (1993), and *Flags of Our Fathers,* in which the dominant fictions of American life are portrayed as both idealizing and disabling.[10] Curnow, for his part, offers an intricate reading of the acting of Bradley Cooper in the title role, finding in his performance degrees of ambivalence and psychological tension that convey something not found on the pages of the memoir, an interior life fretted with self-awareness and perhaps even regret.[11] These critiques, in my view, engage with the film in a nuanced way.

What I am most interested in drawing into view with this chapter, however, is the film's overarching critique of the dominant fiction of the American past as it has been interpreted in twenty-first-century culture. The cult of the gun, the celebration of force, the magnified importance of violence as a reflex response to perceived vulnerability—the codes that have shaped the American national imaginary are explored here as both empowering and destructive. The film's closing narrative scene illustrates the conflict between the mythic memory and the reality of contemporary American life, as Kyle, six-gun in hand, acts the role of a Western gunman, only to be shortly cut down himself by a veteran suffering from PTSD. In a way, the "legend of the formation of the code," as Rancière has described the narrative thrust of the American cinema, is reenacted in this work and embodied in the main character, who carries the nickname "Legend."[12] Chris Kyle, however, is presented as both the avatar and the victim of this mythos. Attempting to embody a certain type of American stoic hero, grimly performing an implacable role that has been inculcated in him by his father, by the SEALs, and by cultural stereotype, Kyle is beset by psychic and moral injury. The national story of the twenty-first century, the film suggests, carries within it a shadow narrative, one that has become increasingly manifest in social, subjective, and cultural life.

CONCLUSION

THE TWENTY-FIRST-CENTURY U.S. WAR FILM, as I have argued in this book, illuminates a changing field of national imaginings, registering with particular vividness the transformation of narratives once thought to be foundational—stories of sacrifice, rescue, brotherhood, and forgiveness. These scripts are retained in genre memory but no longer serve to shape the drama or energize the plot. In the early twenty-first century, the narratives that have traditionally reinforced a sense of national and historic identity in the United States have given way to something else. Although the contested character of contemporary social life and the general loss of confidence in traditional institutions has been much commented on, little has been written about the erosion of narratives of social cohesion articulated in artistic genres, a topic that animates this book. Where Hermann Kappelhoff could convincingly argue that the classic American war film established the "frontlines of community" in the twentieth century, the twenty-first-century war film, I argue, plays a very different role.[1]

With its comparatively long history, the war film serves as a remarkable repository of historical and genre memory. The films I discuss "remember the past," evoking and at times rehearsing certain prominent scenes and war film conventions from earlier periods, even as they mark their distance from them. The metanarratives of nation and sacrifice, disillusionment and loss, which have dominated war cinema for over a century, have become something like ghost paradigms, haunting the text, able to be sensed in certain moments, but no longer viable as structuring principles. What has emerged instead is a new set of motifs, plot configurations, and dramatis personae—particularly visible in the central roles women play in several of these films—that have yet to cohere as a consistent thematic cluster or overarching narrative mode. New, innovative genres of artistic expression growing out of this extraordinarily tumultuous period of American history will surely emerge over time. In this book, I consider the deep, structural changes that are now manifest in an established genre—perhaps the first true genre of film—whose historical importance gives it a particular stature as a bellwether of shifts in cultural and social life.

At the most basic, referential level, the films I treat in this volume dramatize the several ways the so-called war on terror differs from the historical wars of the past. Focusing on conflicts occurring outside the territorial United States, these works convey fundamental departures from the past in several domains of represented conflict, ranging from the way war is conceived, in which the conquering or recovery of contested territory is no longer the goal; to the nature of the enemy, who is often invisible, a shadowy cell of resistance embedded in the population; to the weapons of war, such as the drone, the body bomb, and the IED. These changes also extend to the portrayal of the tactics of war, where today's shock terror attack and clandestine raid are much more the currency of represented violence than yesterday's massed armies on the move.

One of the central premises of this book is that the war on terror, with its absence of temporal and geographic limits, has bled into the U.S. domestic front in an unpredictable and novel way. The mentality of war now shapes much of social and political life in the twenty-first century, exemplified and perhaps reinforced by the extraordinary rise of paramilitary groups, the growing use of secret channels and networks of communication in ostensibly civilian enclaves, and the wild proliferation of weapons among populations convinced that the United States is beset by threats. This is a topic that has not found explicit expression in films, as yet. The contagion of war, the diffusion of violence from declared military conflict zones into the civilian, domestic world, lies just outside the frame of the films I treat in this study. In some works, such as *American Sniper* (2014), it comes directly into view—in disturbing ways.

In parallel to what I have called the collapse of the code—the erosion of the dominant fictions that have sustained a sense of social and national coherence for decades—the narrative structures of the films I consider have changed as well. Narrative form, in my view, provides a particularly resonant expression of the historical imaginary, offering a snapshot, or perhaps an X-ray, of cultural belief and emotion in a specific period. Narrative, as Fredric Jameson has argued, is a "socially symbolic act."[2] Changes in forms of narrative expression can be compared to seismic signals, a coded message of larger changes in historical and cultural life.

The narrative form of the war film, however, at least at first glance, would appear to be an exception. Historically, it has maintained a remarkable stability. Organized teleologically, with a consistent set of narrative moves and a clear-cut set of actants, the war narrative, at the structural level, has changed little since the *Iliad*. This striking observation was first made by Jameson, who notes that war constitutes one of the most celebrated and universal story forms, present in nearly every society over many millennia—a universality that is partly due to the fact that it seems to have a built-in story structure. The agonistic structure of the war story, its delineated actantial roles and well-defined schema of conflict and resolution, suggest a core morphology or syntax and a certain patterned regularity. Considering the enormous transformations in the modes of production, types of weaponry, and profound shifts in artistic media and aesthetic styles over the course of more than two millennia, the fact that the basic structure has changed so little is remarkable. As Jameson says, "One often has the feeling that all war novels (and war films) are pretty much the same and have few enough surprises for us, even though their situations may vary."[3]

In this study, however, I have tried to show how the conventional narrative structure of the war film has been altered. For one, the teleological orientation of war cinema is suspended in many of these films. *The Hurt Locker* (2008), *Zero Dark Thirty* (2011), and *A Private War* (2018), for example, do not begin or conclude in the typical way; the plots begin in medias res, and the conclusions seem to cycle back to an earlier moment or to open to the next set of moves, as if the continuous warfare of the twenty-first century does not lend itself to even a symbolic resolution. The cycling back marks a recursive structure, a repetitive reiteration of moments seen earlier, a device that suggests the ongoing nature of war's violence. In another change, the sorting of characters into the agents and the receivers has also been blurred. In *Eye in the Sky* (2015), *Restrepo* (2010), and *American Sniper,* the agents of war—the soldiers who enact the violence—are cast both as agents and as victims—a striking recoding of actantial relations that I have described in terms of a displacement of affect, a shift of pathos signals from those that have been harmed to those that are the perpetrators of war's violence. This transfer of affect is one of the most distinctive features of the new war films and signals a major change in the way war is represented. As Jonna Eagle points out, a sense of victimization and vulnerability once went hand in hand with punitive agency in American genre forms, providing the motive—or the alibi—for an ultimate assertion of power and dominance. Eagle's perceptive reading of what she calls "imperial affect," however, no longer conveys a sense of generative renewal. Spectacular, retributive violence as a heightened symbolic solution to perceived vulnerability has disappeared as an imaginative frame in the American war film, though maybe not in social and political life.[4] Perhaps the increasing focus on the psychological costs of war, with psychological and moral injury now providing a kind of leitmotif of narratives of war—an emphasis that constitutes a profound change from past representations—has silenced the triumphalism that was once expected in these stories. The displacement of affective signals from the explicit victims of aggression to the soldiers wielding the weapons remains, however, a disturbing attribute of the new war films, one that I have not entirely worked out. Perhaps this will be a question for further research and analysis.

Finally, I would like to note how the home front enters the symbolic discourse of the films I treat in this study. In *American Sniper,* it is portrayed as an illusory world, where images of nature, animals, and children seem to signify stability and order. This pastoral universe is shown to be crosshatched with fear, paranoia, and guilt. The feral violence that has occurred for decades in the wars waged abroad, and the damage it has caused to minds and bodies on both sides, has been superimposed on the American dreamscape, the film suggests, where it lurks, ready to erupt, in moments of perceived threat. In *Eye in the Sky,* the home front is pictured differently, but in a way that is equally fraught. As the young drone pilots report for duty, their base of operations is shown to be a group of trailers stationed in the Nevada desert, each one labeled with the area of the world they control from the sky. Entering these command centers, fresh from their morning coffee, the pilots, a young man and woman, carry out orders handed down from above—sentences of life or death. At the end of the film, following their killing strike, the two pilots exit their trailer, blinking against the harsh Nevada sun, and perhaps blinking back their own emotions. They stand in silence as they receive their instructions to come back, ready for more, in a few hours. The film then concludes with a return shot to Alia, the young Kenyan girl who has been killed in the drone attack in Nairobi, whirling with her toy hoop in her backyard, a reminder of a different home front, a peaceful family environment, that has been devastated in the course of the pilots' workday. And in *Zero Dark Thirty,* the character of Maya, after the killing and identification of bin Laden, is presented with a choice. The pilot of the troop carrier has been instructed to take her anywhere she would like to go. The question lingers, as Maya, in an intense and long-held close-up, cannot seem to give him a destination. The word "home" does not leap to her lips.

More than a natural evolution of genre form, the twenty-first-century war film is marked by a pronounced rewriting of codes and conventions that have persisted, with remarkable consistency, for over a century. Rather than regret, however, or a sense of nostalgia for the striking set pieces and dramas of the past, my own, tentatively hopeful response to this dissolution of the dominant codes of war cinema is that it may signal a positive change, heralding a different future, one that is no longer in thrall to narratives of collective violence, sacrifice, and heroic rescue. If the films that I have tracked in this book can be viewed as the beginning counternarratives to an older mythos of war's violence, particularly its framing as heroic and redemptive, they will have played a consequential and enlightening role.

ACKNOWLEDGMENTS

I was invited to give several presentations on this project at various stages of its evolution, and I wish to thank my hosts and many friends who provided me with the means to sharpen my arguments and see things from new perspectives. Principal among them are Josh Yumibe, Anne Gjelsvik, Michael Wedel, Hermann Kappelhoff, Alan O'Leary, Kim Nelson, Elisabeth Bronfen, and Anelise Corseuil, whose invitations to speak before highly responsive and engaged audiences, and whose own interactions with my work were hugely important to this project's success. Thanks also to Lisa Purse, Catherine Grant, Drehli Robnik, Kevin McSorley, Richard English, Ian Christie, Louis Bayman, and the recently departed Thomas Elsaesser for their interest and encouragement.

The book project was begun with the enthusiastic support of my initial editor at the University of Minnesota Press, Danielle Kasprzak, who was constant in her belief—despite my many revisions, rethinkings, and postponed deadlines—that the project was worth doing. I wish also to thank Leah Pennywark, now my editor at Minnesota, for her excellent ear and for her deep interest in and engagement with the text.

My two external evaluators, Tanine Allison of Emory University and Jonna Eagle of the University of Hawai'i, became major partners in crafting the finished version. Their subtle grasp of the significant points and their excellent, close readings were invaluable. I thank them for their clarity and rigor.

Finally, I wish to thank the doctoral students I have worked with over the years, many of whom developed projects that ran parallel to my own, and whose work helped shape the volume. To John Trafton, Ketlyn Mara Rosa, Chelsea Wessels, Pasquale Cicchetti, and Eileen Rositzka (now departed), please accept my gratitude.

NOTES

INTRODUCTION

1. Anthony D. Smith, "War and Ethnicity: The Role of Warfare in the Formation, Self-Images, and Cohesion of Ethnic Communities," *Ethnic and Racial Studies* 4, no. 4 (1981): 391.

2. Jacques Rancière, "Interview: The Image of Brotherhood," trans. Kari Hanet, *Edinburgh '77 Magazine*, 1977, 26–31.

3. Ibid., 26.

4. Jonna Eagle, *Imperial Affects: Sensational Melodrama and the Attractions of American Cinema* (New Brunswick, N.J.: Rutgers University Press, 2017), 8

5. See Robert Burgoyne, *The Hollywood Historical Film* (Malden, Mass.: Blackwell, 2008); and Burgoyne, *Film Nation: Hollywood Looks at U.S. History*, rev. ed. (Minneapolis: University of Minnesota Press 2010).

6. For a discussion of the concept of genre memory in literature, see Gary Saul Morson and Caryl Emerson, *Mikhail Bakhtin: The Creation of a Prosaics* (Stanford, Calif.: Stanford University Press, 1990), 278.

7. Quoted in ibid., 277.

8. Sarah Cole, *At the Violet Hour: Modernism and Violence in England and Ireland* (Oxford: Oxford University Press, 2012), 81.

9. Yuval Noah Harari, *The Ultimate Experience: Battlefield Revelations and the Making of Modern War Culture, 1450–2000* (Basingstoke, UK: Palgrave Macmillan, 2008).

10. Tanine Allison, *Destructive Sublime: World War II in Contemporary Film and Media* (New Brunswick, N.J.: Rutgers University Press, 2018).

11. Linda Hutcheon, *The Politics of Postmodernism* (London: Routledge, 1989).

12. Harari, *Ultimate Experience*, 7.

13. Gregory, Derek, "The Natures of War," *Antipode*, 48, no. 1 (August 21, 2015), https://doi.org/10.1111/anti.12173.

14. Garrett Stewart, "Digital Fatigue: Imaging War in Recent American Film," *Film Quarterly* 62, no. 4 (2009): 45–55.

15. James Der Derian, *Virtuous War: Mapping the Military-Industrial-Media-Entertainment Network* (London: Routledge, 2001).

16. Yvonne Tasker, *Soldiers' Stories: Military Women in Cinema and Television since World War II* (Durham, N.C.: Duke University Press, 2011).

17. Alisa Lebow, "The Unwar Film," in *A Companion to Contemporary Documentary Film*, ed. Alexandra Juhasz and Alisa Lebow (Malden, Mass.: Wiley Blackwell, 2015), 454–74.

18. Kristin Whissel, "The Gender of Empire," in *A Feminist Reader in Early Cinema*, ed. Jennifer M. Bean and Diane Negra (Durham, N.C.: Duke University Press, 2002), 141–65.

19. Saumava Mitra, "Revisiting *Restrepo*: The Men and Boys beyond the Wire," presentation given at the Tim Hetherington Collection and Conflict Imagery Research Network launch event, April 22, 2021.

1. EMBODIMENT AND PATHOS IN THE WAR FILM

1. Chris Hedges, *War Is a Force That Gives Us Meaning* (New York: PublicAffairs, 2002).

2. Thomas Elsaesser, "*Zero Dark Thirty*: Genre Hybridization as (Parapractic) Interference," in *The Mind Game Film: Distributed Agency, Time Travel, and Productive Pathology*, ed. Thomas Elsaesser, Warren Buckland, Dana Polan, and Seung-hoon Jeong (New York: Routledge, 2021), 224–44.

3. Kevin McSorley, "Helmetcams, Militarized Sensation, and 'Somatic War,'" *Journal of War and Culture Studies* 5, no. 1 (2012): 47–58.

4. Kevin McDonald, "Grammars of Violence, Modes of Embodiment, and Frontiers of the Subject," in *War and the Body: Militarisation, Practice and Experience*, ed. Kevin McSorley (London: Routledge, 2013), 138–51.

5. Gary Saul Morson and Caryl Emerson, *Mikhail Bakhtin: Creation of a Prosaics* (Stanford, Calif.: Stanford University Press, 1990), 297.

6. Hermann Kappelhoff, *Front Lines of Community: Hollywood between War and Democracy*, trans. Daniel Hendrickson (Berlin: De Gruyter, 2018), 7.

7. Hermann Kappelhoff, "For Love of Country: World War II in Hollywood Cinema at the Turn of the Century" (unpublished manuscript; English translation supplied by the author, 2012).

8. Kappelhoff, *Front Lines of Community*, 133.

9. Elsaesser, "*Zero Dark Thirty*," 232.

10. Ibid., 233.

11. For an extended comparison of the two films and their lead

characters, see John Trafton, "'Things that almost killed me': *Apocalypse Now, The Hurt Locker,* and the Influence of 19th Century Spectacle Art in the War Film," *Frames Cinema Journal,* no. 2 (November 21, 2012), http://frames cinemajournal.com/article/things-that-almost-killed-me-apocalypse-now-and-the-hurt-locker-and-the-influence-of-19th-century-spectacle-art-in-the-war-film/.

12. Ibid.

13. Douglas A. Cunningham, "Explosive Structure: Fragmenting the New Modernist War Narrative in *The Hurt Locker,*" *CineAction* 81 (Summer 2010), http://www.cineaction.ca/order/81-war-films-female-directors/.

14. Elaine Scarry, *The Body in Pain: The Making and Unmaking of the World* (New York: Oxford University Press, 1987), 137.

15. Thomas Elsaesser, "Retrospektion, Überlebensschuld und affektives Gedächtnis: *Saving Private Ryan,*" in *Korper, Tod Und Technik Metamorphosen Des Kriegfilms,* ed. Thomas Elsaesser and Michael Wedel (Paderborn: Konstanz University Press, 2016), 65–102.

16. Robert Eberwein, *The Hollywood War Film* (Boston: Wiley Blackwell, 2009).

17. Benedict Anderson, *Imagined Communities: Reflections on the Origin and Spread of Nationalism* (London: Verso, 1991).

18. Fredric Jameson, *The Political Unconscious: Narrative as a Socially Symbolic Act* (Ithaca, N.Y.: Cornell University Press, 1981), 35.

2. WAITING FOR TERROR

1. Sarah Cole, *At the Violet Hour: Modernism and Violence in England and Ireland* (Oxford: Oxford University Press, 2012), 4.

2. Jonna Eagle, *Imperial Affects: Sensational Melodrama and the Attractions of American Cinema* (New Brunswick, N.J.: Rutgers University Press, 2017). Eagle's study puts the concept of wounded potency and retributive violence into a larger context. The history of imperialist violence throughout the twentieth century, in her reading, is animated precisely by a sense of crisis, where injury and suffering are linked to the mobilization of violent agency. She argues that mainstream cultural forms of the twentieth century, including the action film and the Western, have created and reinforced a pattern of affective response in the spectator that translates into a widespread social disposition. Eagle sees vulnerability and violent action as twinned experiences in American culture, a motivated and conventional pairing. The violence of the American empire in the twenty-first century, she maintains, comes with a well-rehearsed set of antecedents. The "national subject," conditioned by the signifying modes of action melodrama, is constituted as both vulnerable and invincible, wounded and all-powerful.

Nationalist violence, she writes, "is produced as both righteous and retributive, always already defensive in nature" (6).

3. Cole, *At the Violet Hour,* 287.

4. Anne McClintock, "Paranoid Empire: Specters from Guantánamo and Abu Ghraib," *Small Axe* 13, no. 1 (2009): 57.

5. Paul Virilio, *War and Cinema: The Logistics of Perception,* trans. Patrick Camiller (London: Verso, 1992), 5.

6. For a very different reading of Maya's role, the torture scenes depicted in the work, and the film as a whole, see Guy Westwell, *Parallel Lines: Post-9/11 American Cinema* (New York: Wallflower Press, 2014), 172–78. Westwell sees the film as essentially conservative and recuperative, emphasizing aspects of the work that present a "curtailed version of history, a rigorously unilateral and sympathetic point of view and, ultimately, closure" (178).

7. The torture scenes in *Zero Dark Thirty* have catalyzed a wide-ranging debate about torture as policy and practice during the early years of the war on terror, especially its effectiveness or its limitations in gathering useful information, and the particular role that torture played in uncovering the location of bin Laden in Pakistan. The larger question concerning the morality of torture, specifically whether it is justified even if the lives of innocents might be at stake, has received much less discussion. Generating perhaps the most heated political response to a film since Oliver Stone's *JFK* (1991), the torture sequences in *Zero Dark Thirty* provoked intensive controversy even before the actual release of the film. Senator Carl Levin, the head of the Appropriations Committee, and Senators Diane Feinstein and John McCain, members of the Senate Oversight Committee—all of whom had access to top secret documents detailing the CIA's practices—insisted the film was misleading and false in the connection it drew between torture and the discovery of the nom de guerre of bin Laden's courier. The acting director of the CIA, Michael Morrell, similarly chastised the filmmakers for implying that torture was instrumental in supplying the initial leads to bin Laden's location, arguing that the successful search for bin Laden was in no way informed by or dependent on torture. Many journalists and cultural commentators similarly denounced the film, claiming that its depictions amount to a "pro-torture" argument. Other prominent writers and filmmakers, however, including the filmmaker Michael Moore, extolled its integrity in detailing the physical reality of torture as practiced by the United States during the early war on terror, the CIA's use of black sites, and its practice of extraordinary rendition. These writers and commentators emphasized the film's frankness in dealing with this sordid chapter in American history, bringing to wide visibility the institutional practice of torture by both U.S. personnel and foreign governments under U.S. influence.

Perhaps the most balanced, and to my mind, informed account of the torture controversy is an opinion piece in *The Atlantic* by Mark Bowden, "*Zero Dark Thirty* Is Not Pro-Torture," January 3, 2013, https://www.theatlantic.com/entertainment/archive/2013/01/zero-dark-thirty-is-not-pro-torture/266759/. Bowden counters the reading given by so many of the film's critics—that the film is morally tainted because torture is depicted as effective—by underlining the two key instances in the film in which torture is demonstrated as failing to elicit good information—the initial torture scene of Ammar, at the beginning of the film, in which he does not reveal the date of an imminent attack in Saudi Arabia, despite extreme pressure; and the later torture of the high-level operative, Khalid Sheikh Mohammed, who provides only false information. Rather than showing that the actual infliction of torture was instrumental in gaining critical information, the film depicts, with appalling accuracy, a culture in which torture forms the background and sets the terms of all the interrogations that take place. One high-level captive in the film, for example, says he will cooperate because he "has no desire to be tortured again." Another lies even after being waterboarded several times. His determination to conceal the identity of the courier, even under extreme and repeated duress, is taken by Maya as confirmation of the courier's importance. The film details, with uncompromising directness, an institutional culture defined by physical violence in the early period of the war on terror.

The argument that the film is pro-torture, that it posits—and seems to endorse—a link between brutal interrogation and the revelations that led to bin Laden, is also contradicted by the mise-en-scène of these sequences. The desolate, washed-out color scheme, the harsh lighting, the squalid interrogation cells, the blood and urine on the floor, the battered, swollen features of the detainee—the visual and acoustic signals the torture scenes emit are concentrated expressions of violence in its most disenchanted form. Here, the language of cinema, its specific forms of expression, shapes the meaning of these scenes and provides an index of the film's complex political stance. The realistic depiction of torture as it appears in *Zero Dark Thirty*—the act of showing torture in an unvarnished way—carries a potent negative charge. The visual design of the scenes, the stress positions and figure behavior of the detainees and the interrogators, as well as the cinematography and shot patterning situate the violence of torture in a zone of institutional pathology more familiar from the depictions of the Nazis in films such as *Rome, Open City* (dir. Roberto Rossellini, 1946) or the French colonial police in *The Battle of Algiers* (dir. Gillo Pontecorvo, 1966).

8. Slavoj Žižek, "*Zero Dark Thirty:* Hollywood's Gift to American Power," *The Guardian*, January 25, 2013, https://www.theguardian.com/co

mmentisfree/2013/jan/25/zero-dark-thirty-normalises-torture-unjustifiable.

9. Cole, *At the Violet Hour*, 43, 81.

10. Eileen Rositzka, *Cinematic Corpographies: Re-Mapping the War Film through the Body* (Berlin: De Gruyter, 2018), 163.

11. See Fredric Jameson, *The Political Unconscious: Narrative as a Socially Symbolic Act* (Ithaca, N.Y.: Cornell University Press, 1981).

12. Steven Shaviro, "A Brief Remark on *Zero Dark Thirty*," *Pinocchio Theory* (blog), January 18, 2013, http://www.shaviro.com/Blog/?p=1114.

13. Ibid.

14. Mark Bowden, *The Finish: The Killing of Osama bin Laden* (New York: Atlantic Monthly Press, 2012), 98, 107.

15. Tricia Jenkins and Tony Shaw, "From Zero to Hero: The CIA and Hollywood Today," *Cinema Journal* 56, no. 2 (2017): 95.

16. Sarah Cole, "Enchantment, Disenchantment, War, Literature," *PMLA* 124, no. 5 (2009): 1636.

17. Cole argues that literature engages with violence at a deep aesthetic level—it neither "flees violence, nor transcends it," she writes, but rather "trades on its power"—a perspective that is useful for considering the semiotics of violence in *Zero Dark Thirty* (ibid., 1645). Enchanted violence, in her words, "refers to the tendency to see in violence some kind of transformative power . . . [it] relies primarily on metaphors of growth and germination; it steers as far from the violated body as it can" (1633–34). Centered primarily on Modernist writers whose work was shaped by the horrors of World War I, her analysis also extends to the *Iliad*—perhaps the original war narrative—and in a different direction to the work of Frantz Fanon. The anti-colonial, emancipatory writing of Fanon, for example, is suffused with appeals to enchanted violence. In Fanon's words, "At the individual level, violence is a cleansing force. It rids the colonized of their inferiority complex, of their passive and despairing attitude" (51). And "the colonized man liberates himself in and through violence" (44). See *The Wretched of the Earth*, trans. Richard Philcox (New York: Grove, 2004). As Cole summarizes, "The infectious, celebratory quality of Fanon's rhetoric about the power of violence to remake history and the individual . . . might be viewed as a signature . . . for any theory of generative violence" (1636). For most of the writers Cole considers, the imagery of enchantment and disenchantment is complexly intertwined, producing a "combined aura of celebration and devastation" (*At the Violet Hour*, 39, 43, 81).

18. Andrew Hill, "The bin Laden Tapes," in *Covering Bin Laden: Global Media and the World's Most Wanted Man*, ed. Susan Jeffords and Fahed Al-Sumait (Champaign: University of Illinois Press, 2015), 45–46.

19. Bigelow's earlier film, *Blue Steel* (1990), ends in a similar way, with an extended close-up of the main character, Megan Turner (Jamie Lee Curtis), a female cop, sitting alone in her squad car.

20. Richard Jackson, "Bin Laden's Ghost and the Epistemological Crises of Counterterrorism," in *Covering Bin Laden*, 10.

21. Ibid., 14.

3. INTIMATE VIOLENCE

1. Yuval Noah Harari, *The Ultimate Experience: Battlefield Revelations and the Making of Modern War Culture, 1450–2000* (Basingstoke, UK: Palgrave Macmillan, 2008).

2. Mark Bowden, "The Killing Machines: How to Think about Drones," *The Atlantic*, September 2013, https://www.theatlantic.com/magazine/archive/2013/09/the-killing-machines-how-to-think-about-drones/309434/.

3. Eyal Weitzman, *The Least of All Possible Evils: Humanitarian Violence from Arendt to Gaza* (London: Verso, 2011).

4. Grégoire Chamayou, *A Theory of the Drone*, trans. Janet Lloyd (New York: The New Press, 2015), 53.

5. Ibid., 44.

6. Ibid., 57.

7. Tanine Allison, *Destructive Sublime: World War II in American Film and Media* (New Brunswick, N.J.: Rutgers University Press, 2018).

8. Harun Farocki, "Phantom Images," *Public* 29 (2004): 17. A gloss on this essay is provided by Chamayou in *Theory of the Drone*, 114.

9. Giacomo Balla, Benedetta, Fortunato Depero, Gerardo Dottori, Fillia, F. T. Marinetti, Enrico Prampolini, Mino Somenzi, and Tato, "Manifesto of Aeropainting," in *Futurism: An Anthology*, ed. Lawrence Rainey, Christine Poggi, and Laura Wittman (New Haven, Conn.: Yale University Press, 2009), 283–86.

10. Chamayou, *Theory of the Drone*, 55.

11. Garrett Stewart, "Digital Fatigue: Imaging War in Recent American Film," *Film Quarterly* 62, no. 4 (Summer 2009): 45.

12. Chamayou, *Theory of the Drone*, 56.

13. Derek Gregory, "Moving Targets and Violent Cartographies," July 2012, https://geographicalimaginations.files.wordpress.com/2012/07/derek-gregory-moving-targets-and-violent-geographies-final.pdf.

14. Derek Gregory, "From a View to a Kill: Drones and Late Modern War," *Theory Culture Society* 28 (2012): 188.

15. Ibid., 196.

16. Lilie Chouliaraki, "Digital Witnessing in Conflict Zones: The Politics

of Remediation," *Information, Communication, and Society*, 18, no. 11 (2015): 1362–77.

17. Gregory, "From a View to a Kill," 193.

18. NBC News, "Huge Portrait of Pakistani Girl Takes Aim at Drone Operators," April 8, 2014, https://www.nbcnews.com/news/world/huge-portrait-pakistani-girl-takes-aim-drone-operators-n74481.

19. Harari, *Ultimate Experience*.

20. See Patricia Pisters, "Logistics of Perception 2.0: Multiple Screen Aesthetics in Iraq War Films," *Film-Philosophy* 14, no. 1 (2010): 232–52. See also Stewart, "Digital Fatigue."

21. Chamayou, *Theory of the Drone*, 139.

22. Lisa Parks, "Drones, Vertical Mediation, and the Targeted Class," *Feminist Studies* 42, no. 1 (2016): 227.

23. Derek Gregory, "Darkness Descending," *Geographical Imaginations* (blog), July 29, 2014, https://geographicalimaginations.com/2014/07/29/darkness-descending/.

24. Nasser Hussain, "The Sound of Terror: Phenomenology of a Drone Strike," *Boston Review*, October 16, 2013, http://www.bostonreview.net/world/hussain-drone-phenomenology.

25. Sarah Cole, *At the Violet Hour: Modernism and Violence in England and Ireland* (Oxford: Oxford University Press, 2012), 43.

26. Weizman, *Least of All Possible Evils*, 6.

27. Ibid., 10.

4. WAR AS REVELATION

1. Marie Colvin, "Bravery Is Not Being Afraid to Be Afraid," *Sunday Times*, October 21, 2001. Although Colvin writes that war has not fundamentally changed in over one hundred years, what has changed is the targeting of journalists for assassination, a dramatic shift in the rules and conventions of the battlefront. Although it is not uncommon for journalists to be killed in war zones, an increasing number of these deaths are intentional, the result of the specific targeting of reporters and photographers. According to the Committee to Protect Journalists, in the year 2020, for example, some thirty-two journalists were confirmed murdered. From 1992 to 2021, 1,402 journalists have been confirmed murdered. The targeting of journalists, occurring both in both active war zones and in civilian settings in Europe and North America, is a dimension of contemporary conflict that has not, until now, been represented in film or in any other narrative form. See "2180 Journalists and Media Workers Killed between 1992 and 2022: Motive Confirmed or Unconfirmed," Committee to Project Journalists, accessed November 3, 2022, https://cpj.org/data/killed/?status=Killed&motiveCon

firmed%5B%5D=Confirmed&motiveUnconfirmed%5B%5D=Unconfirmed&type%5B%5D=Journalist&type%5B%5D=Media%20Worker&start_year=1992&end_year=2022&group_by=year.

2. Robert Burgoyne, *Film Nation: Hollywood Looks at U.S. History*, rev. ed. (Minneapolis: University of Minnesota Press, 2010).

3. Marie Brenner, "Marie Colvin's Private War," *Vanity Fair*, July 18, 2012.

4. Yuval Noah Harari, *The Ultimate Experience: Battlefield Revelations and the Making of Modern War Culture, 1450–2000* (Basingstoke, UK: Palgrave Macmillan, 2008), 7.

5. Ibid., 7–8.

6. William Guynn, *Unspeakable Histories: Film and the Experience of Catastrophe* (New York: Columbia University Press, 2016).

7. Penelope Poulou, "*A Private War* Underscores Risks Journalists Take," VOA, November 16, 2018, https://www.voanews.com/a/a-private-war-underscores-risks-journalists-take/4662110.html.

8. The historian Yuval Noah Harari writes that the idea of war as truth, of war as revelation, has dominated the Western understanding of war for the past two centuries: "Western culture still attaches one supremely positive value to war. Deep within late modern Western culture, the association between war and truth is hammered again and again. The master narratives of late modern war all agree that war reveals eternal truths—even if weakness prevents people from facing them" (*Ultimate Experience*, 305).

9. In the actual, historical interview, cell phone footage of the death of a child, taken from YouTube, dominates the broadcast—a different video than what Conroy had recorded in the triage area in the film. In the historical broadcast, a baby is seen dying on camera—a graphic, difficult-to-watch scene. This video did not originate with Colvin and Conroy; it had been had been uploaded to YouTube some days earlier. In the historical interview, Anderson Cooper blurs the provenance of the video, giving the impression that it could be the reportage of Colvin and Conroy. And in the actual interview, the real-life Colvin allowed this impression to stand. As Lindsey Hilsum points out in her biography, *In Extremis: The Life and Death of the War Correspondent Marie Colvin* (New York: Farrar, Strauss and Giroux, 2018), 338–39, Colvin was not in the room. For an insightful analysis of the truth claims of what has come to be known as "digital witnessing" or "citizen journalism," see Lilie Chouliaraki, "Digital Witnessing in Conflict Zones: The Politics of Remediation," *Information, Communication, and Society* 18, no. 11 (2015): 1362–77.

10. In 2019, a U.S. court ordered the Syrian government to pay the family of Marie Colvin $302.5 million for her killing. As the *New York Times* reports, "The plaintiffs detailed, through government records and defectors' and

other witnesses' accounts, how the Syrian government had made a policy of cracking down on journalists and their assistants; how security officials tracked Ms. Colvin through informants and intercepted communications; how Syrian forces killed Ms. Colvin, hours after her last broadcast from Homs, by shelling the makeshift media center where she was staying; and how officials celebrated her death." See Anne Barnard, "Syria Ordered to Pay $302.5 Million to Family of Marie Colvin," *New York Times*, January 31, 2019. See also Anne Barnard, "Syrian Forces Aimed to Kill Journalists, U.S. Court Is Told," *New York Times*, April 9, 2018; and "Marie Colvin's Last Call to CNN," CNN, February 22, 2012, https://www.cnn.com/videos/world/2012/02/22/ac-marie-colvin-syria-baby-dies.cnn.

11. Elisabeth Bronfen, *Specters of War: Hollywood's Engagement with Military Conflict* (New Brunswick, N.J.: Rutgers University Press, 2012), 1.

5. FOUR ELEGIES OF WAR

1. Alisa Lebow, "The Unwar Film," in *A Companion to Contemporary Documentary Film*, ed. Alexandra Juhasz and Alisa Lebow (Malden, Mass.: Wiley Blackwell, 2015), 454–74.

2. Erina Duganne, "Uneasy Witnesses: Broomberg, Chanarin, and Photojournalism's Expanded Field," in *Getting the Picture: The Visual Culture of the News*, ed. Jason E. Hill and Vanessa R. Schwartz (London: Bloomsbury, 2015), 272–79.

3. Ibid., 279.

4. Saumava Mitra, "Revisiting *Restrepo*: The Men and Boys beyond the Wire," presentation given at the Tim Hetherington Collection and Conflict Imagery Research Network launch event, April 22, 2021.

5. Robert Burgoyne, *Film Nation: Hollywood Looks at U.S. History*, rev. (Minneapolis, University of Minnesota Press, 2010).

6. Kristin Whissel, "The Gender of Empire," in *A Feminist Reader in Early Cinema*, ed. Jennifer M. Bean and Diane Negra (Durham, N.C.: Duke University Press, 2002), 141–65.

7. Tim Hetherington, "By Any Means Necessary," *Foto8* (blog), May 9, 2008, https://www.foto8.com/live/by-any-means-necessary/.

8. Thomas Elsaesser, "Retrospektion, Überlebensschuld und affektives Gedächtnis: *Saving Private Ryan*," in *Korper, Tod Und Technik Metamorphosen Des Kriegfilms*, ed. Thomas Elsaesser and Michael Wedel (Paderborn: Konstanz University Press, 2016), 65–102.

9. Paul Fussell, *The Great War and Modern Memory* (Oxford: Oxford University Press, 1975).

10. Lilie Chouliaraki, "Authoring the Self: Media, Voice, and Testimony in Soldiers' Memoires," *Media, War, and Conflict* 8, no. 4 (2016): 58–75.

11. Sebastian Junger, dir., *Which Way is the Front Line from Here? The Life and Times of Tim Hetherington* (London: Goldcrest Films International, 2013), DVD.

12. Robert Burgoyne and Eileen Rositzka, "Goya on His Shoulder: Tim Hetherington, Genre Memory, and the Body at Risk," *Frames Cinema Journal*, 2015, http://framescinemajournal.com/article/goya-on-his-shoulder-tim-hetherington-genre-memory-and-the-body-at-risk/.

13. Adam Broomberg and Oliver Chanarin, "Indifferent but Not Unconcerned," *Foto8* (blog), May 5, 2008, https://static1.squarespace.com/static/56e1e3e24d088e6834d4fbf4/t/57a1feb1d482e9ab0a398d48/1494958009521/TEXT+-+Unconcerned+But+Not+Indifferent.

14. Duganne, "Uneasy Witnesses," 277.

15. Sebastian Junger, "How PTSD Became a Problem Far beyond the Battlefield," *Vanity Fair*, June 2015, http://www.vanityfair.com/news/2015/05/ptsd-war-home-sebastian-junger.

16. Mitra, "Revisiting *Restrepo*."

17. Sebastian Junger in *Infidel*, by Tim Hetherington (London: Chris Boot, 2010).

18. Duganne, "Uneasy Witnesses," 277.

19. Francesco Casetti, "Mapping the Sensible: Distribution, Inscription, Cinematic Thinking," presentation at the Digital Cinepoetics Workshop, November 18, 2020. Casetti's point was made during the public discussion portion of the workshop.

6. AMERICAN PASTORAL

1. Jonna Eagle, *War Games* (New Brunswick, N.J.: Rutgers University Press, 2019), 104–5.

2. Loosely based on Chris Kyle's 2013 autobiography *American Sniper: The Autobiography of the Most Lethal Sniper in U.S. Military History*, the film departs significantly from the memoir in tone, theme, and structure. In an unpublished work, James Curnow details the film's adherence to and departures from the conventions of the biopic, closely analyzing the dialog the film establishes with the source material. See "No Such Thing as Heroes: Clint Eastwood, Metahistorian" (PhD diss., Monash University, April 2021).

3. Gerard Genette, *Narrative Discourse: An Essay in Method*, trans. Jane E. Lewin (Ithaca, N.Y.: Cornell University Press, 1980).

4. Sigmund Freud, "A Child Is Being Beaten," in *The Standard Edition of the Complete Psychological Works of Sigmund Freud*, trans. James Strachey with Alix Strachey and Alan Tyson (New York: Vintage, 1999), 17:179–204.

5. Pierre Sorlin, "Cinema and the Memory of the Great War," in *The First World War and Popular Cinema: 1914 to the Present*, ed. Michael Paris (Edinburgh: Edinburgh University Press, 1999), 5–26.

6. Roger Stahl, *Through the Crosshairs: War, Visual Culture, and the Weaponized Gaze* (New Brunswick, N.J.: Rutgers University Press, 2018), 107.

7. Paul Virilio, *War and Cinema: The Logistics of Perception*, trans. Patrick Camiller (London: Verso, 1989).

8. Stahl, *Through the Crosshairs*, 104–5.

9. Eliana Dockterman, "Clint Eastwood Says *American Sniper* Is Anti-War," *Time*, March 17, 2015, https://time.com/3747428/clint-eastwood-american-sniper-anti-war/.

10. Vito Zagarrio, "'The true story that inspired the movie': Cinema, Literature, and History in the Digital Age," *RSA Journal* 26 (2015): 19–38.

11. Curnow, "No Such Thing as Heroes."

12. Jacques Rancière, "Interview: The Image of Brotherhood," trans. Kari Hanet, *Edinburgh '77 Magazine*, 1977, 26.

CONCLUSION

1. Hermann Kappelhoff, *Front Lines of Community: Hollywood between War and Democracy*, trans. Daniel Hendrickson (Berlin: De Gruyter, 2018).

2. Fredric Jameson, *The Political Unconscious: Narrative as a Socially Symbolic Act* (Ithaca, N.Y.: Cornell University Press, 1981).

3. Fredric Jameson, "War and Representation," in "Special Topic: War," special issue, *PMLA* 124, no. 5 (October 2009): 1532–47.

4. Jonna Eagle, *Imperial Affects: Sensational Melodrama and the Attractions of American Cinema* (New Brunswick, N.J.: Rutgers University Press, 2017).

INDEX

Robert Burgoyne is a writer and lecturer. He is author of *Bertolucci's 1900: A Narrative and Historical Analysis; Film Nation: Hollywood Looks at U.S. History, Revised Edition* (Minnesota, 2010); *The Hollywood Historical Film;* coauthor of *New Vocabularies in Film Semiotics: Structuralism, Post-Structuralism, and Beyond*; and editor of *The Epic Film in World Culture* and coeditor of *Refugees and Migrants in Contemporary Film, Art, and Media.*

Made in United States
Troutdale, OR
12/13/2024

26463793R00106